Dating FABRICS

A COLOR GUIDE 1800 - 1960

by Eileen Jahnke Trestain

American Quilter's Society
P.O. Box 3290 • Paducah, KY 42002-3290

Located in Paducah, Kentucky, the American Quilter's Society (AQS), is dedicated to promoting the accomplishments of today's quilters. Through its publications and events, AQS strives to honor today's quilt-makers and their work — and to inspire future creativity and innovation in quiltmaking.

EDITOR: BARBARA SMITH
BOOK DESIGN: ANGELA SCHADE
COVER DESIGN: MICHAEL BUCKINGHAM

Library of Congress Cataloging-in-Publication Data
Trestain, Eileen Jahnke
      Dating fabrics: a color guide (1800–1960) / Eileen Jahnke Trestain
               p.   cm.
      Includes bibliographical references (p. 195–199).
      ISBN 0-89145-884-0
      1. Color in textile industries--Dating.   2. Quilts--United States.
                          I. Title.
NK9112.T76   1998
746.46'0973--dc21   98-29165
                                           CIP

Additional copies of this book may be ordered from: American Quilter's Society, PO Box 3290, Paducah, KY 42002-3290 @ $24.95. Add $2.00 for postage and handling.

Printed in the U.S.A. by Image Graphics, Paducah, KY

DEDICATION

I dedicate this book to my grandmothers Jessie Stowers Hertel, who gave me my quilting beginnings, and Frances Boulard Sislock, who believed in me...

and to my children, Patricia and Carolina, who I hope will understand and share my love of quilting someday.

ACKNOWLEDGMENTS

This book would not be complete without the grateful acknowledgment my friends and colleagues are due. I might never have begun without the encouragement of my friends, particularly the Bits and Pieces group from the Quilter's Guild of Plano, Texas, who encouraged me to follow my dreams. I also thank my friend, Sharon Newman, who has given me so much encouragement. Some special quilt dealers have been invaluable to me including Nancy Kirk and her staff, Joe and Mary Koval, Dianne Reese, John Sauls and his staff, Mary Ann Walters, and Bill Wivel, and the unknown and unnamed antique dealers from whom I have gleaned my collection. In addition, members of the Quilt Restoration Society have been generous in providing samples of early 1800s fabrics, without which this book would definitely be lacking. Most of all, there is my husband, Dave, who has endured with me over the years and had the faith that he could find me wherever there were piles of fabric.

CONTENTS

INTRODUCTION

As a quilt appraiser, I am often asked about the date of origin of the quilts and fabrics I see. I love old quilts, and the fabrics hold a special interest for me. I teach and lecture on this subject and have helped educate a number of people about my beloved old fabrics. However, I cannot be with every quilt or fabric enthusiast who is out in the field, the flea market, garage sale, or quilt show, no matter how much I'd like to.

So I had an idea to prepare a guide book. Since I have been collecting antique fabrics for some time and was the lucky inheritor of my grandmother's collection, I have a lot of fabric samples to share. And it was a great excuse to go out and find more fabric. Isn't that the goal of every quilter, after all? (I'm sure most of our spouses think so.) And we all know, it is not just the purchase of that great old unappreciated treasure that stirs our blood…it is the thrill of the hunt.

Perhaps you are an antique dealer who would like to know more about the cloth or quilt you are trying to sell, an appraiser who has a question to answer about a specific fabric type, or a novice who would like to know a little more about the antique you are thinking of buying or have luckily inherited. I hope this book will help in your quest to learn about and appreciate antique fabrics and their use in quilts and clothing. In any case, happy hunting, and be sure to leave a little bit here and there for the rest of us to find.

HOW TO USE THIS BOOK

I had a bit of a dilemma about the best way to make this book most helpful. I had a choice of dividing the fabrics by color or by time period. If I were to separate by color, then you would see how the individual colors have changed over the years, but if I were to divide by date, then you could eventually become familiar with the colors that were popular in a given era, just by using the book. To include the wisdom of both approaches, I decided to divide by time period and subdivide by color families within that period.

If you know an approximate date, you can turn to that section in the book and compare the colors and print styles to the ones in the item you are examining. Most of these periods have particular colors and styles that were predominant, though an occasional holdover from another period may appear. Quilts and textiles are dated by the most recent fabric in them. So keep in mind that any quilt or textile item cannot be any older than the newest fabric used in it, though parts of it may be much older. If the fabric was printed during more than one period, date the object within the field of time that is supported by the evidence of the other fabrics. Look for repairs with fabrics from an inappropriate time frame. They tend to stand out from the rest.

Whenever possible, I have used fabrics that show no signs of color loss. However, seeing a fabric in the process of fading because of fugitive dyes may be helpful in identifying such pieces, so I have included some faded samples. A swatch may be included under the color it once was, the color it is now, or possibly both. This addition should be particularly helpful for fabrics that are rarely seen in the original color, typically purples, greens, and some pinks.

Due to the processes required to publish a photo in a book, which is very different from dying fabric, some colors printed here may not exactly match the original fabrics. The AQS staff has worked hard to be as accurate as possible in recreating the fabric colors within the constraints of the print medium. Please forgive these minor discrepancies and know that we did the best we could. When in doubt as to the accuracy of any colored print, refer to the text and the style of the print in question to try to verify fabric dates.

Since early fabrics were rarely printed with dates on the fabric itself, I was dependent on my own skills, and those of others who were knowledgeable, to date some of the earliest fabrics in this book. Pre-1800 fabrics are rarely seen outside private collections and museums. Pre-1830 fabrics can be difficult to find unless you live along the Eastern sea-board, and even then, findings are by odd chance. Quilt dealers and repairers collect such fabrics, but they are understandably reluctant to part with these treasures.

The fabrics are printed actual size because altered scale could be confusing. Some manufacturers of reproduction fabrics have altered the scale of the original prints, but with little change in shape and with closely matching color tones. The only way to tell the reproductions from the real thing, especially after artificial aging, is by the quality of the fabrics, close examination of the weave under a magnifier, the feel of the cloth, and examining the wrong side.

I intended for this book to be a practical guide rather than a scholarly treatise on textiles. Some wonderful textbooks have already been written on the subject, for which I am grateful. I recommend that you take time to read some of the books in the bibliography and then go out and practice a little on your own. A glossary has been included to help readers with unfamiliar terms. Also listed in the back of the book are antique quilt and textile dealers who have gone out of their way to help me over the years. I have found these dealers to be honest, truthful, and generous in assisting me in my great hunt, and I feel confident you will also appreciate them.

A NEW NATION

ABOUT THE PERIOD

Quilts and fabrics from this period are rare, and it is difficult to find them other than in museums and private collections. Occasionally, a wondrous surprise appears at a quilt show dealer's booth or an estate sale. Because the fabrics are difficult to find, photographs, museum pieces, and occasional lucky finds are your best bets for familiarizing yourself with these treasures. Because of the rarity of fabrics from this period, some of the prints shown here have been reproduced from color copies of quilts belonging to private owners.

Cotton did not come into great use in Europe and America until the middle to the end of the 1700s. Linen, wool, and silk were the main fabric staples. People from the Asian continent, primarily India, had already developed the skills to produce finely woven and printed cotton and had been doing exactly that for a thousand years or more. It was not until the late 1700s and early 1800s that the American continent was able to produce a great enough quantity of cotton to supply much of the European and American markets.

Much of our early fabric used in American quilts was imported from Europe. Because of restrictions and pressure from European rule, American textile manufacturing was limited. Skilled textile workers were forbidden to migrate to the Americas because textile production was one of the most valuable and necessary elements of society. As long as textile production was controlled by European governments, a great deal of influence on American society was held by the ruling body. Some of the first skilled American textile workers escaped from Europe under false pretenses.

Early textile production and dyeing in the Americas were often home arts, though professional weavers, dyers, and textile printers did occasionally advertise in newspapers and handbills. Many communities had a person known for their dyeing skills, which had been learned through apprenticeship.

In 1790, Samuel Slater came to America as a young man. He had apprenticed in an English textile mill and was able to re-create machinery from memory, which enabled him to begin textile production in the Pawtucket, Rhode Island, area. Soon, other textile ventures followed.

In 1793, Eli Whitney developed the cotton gin, which sped up the process of separating the seed from the cotton filament. Previously, a long, tedious process had been required to hand separate the seed and cotton lint.

A few years later, Francis Cabot Lowell visited England and returned with ideas and plans for powered looms. He established a business, known as the Boston Manufacturing Company, in the Merrimac Valley of Massachusetts. American textile production was up and running full time.

TEXTILE COLORS

Colors from this period are far more varied than often presumed by many beginning fabric aficionados. Some of the early floral prints from India, and later from Europe, were made by a long, involved process, which created a whole spectrum of colors in one print. The steps involved transferring the pattern, outlining the design with a hand-painted (known as penciled) black, then hand block-printed with various mordants. The fabric was then dyed in a madder solution, which created reds, oranges, pinks, blacks, purples, or browns in combination with different mordants. After that, the fabric was sun bleached on grass fields. This process took several weeks or months depending on the weather. When the bleaching was finished, a resist of starchy paste or wax was applied to protect the design from vat dyeing with indigo blue. After the fabric was dyed and the resist removed, yellow was penciled over the blue to make green. Yellow highlights were sometimes added. It could take several months to complete a printed length of yardage. Though simpler and more precise processes were developed during the 1700s, some of the fabric manufacturers continued with the long process in some form.

Indigo blue was one of the earliest known dependable dye colors. According to Susan Boscene in her book *Hand Block Printing & Resist Dyeing*, 13 different shades of indigo were common during the 1700s. Elijah Bemiss in his text of 1815, *The Dyers Companion* (reprinted by Dover books, 1973), devotes an entire, rather lengthy chapter to methods of dyeing with indigo and woad. Indigo was used as a solid vat-dyed color or as a background (ground) for additional printing.

It was fairly common to print indigo over a resist, which created a white design (known as a blue resist). Another design element was added by printing yellow over the blue, creating a textured surface. This yellow was developed from the yellow paints used for carriage trim. Some yellow and blue combinations were created with yellow dye as opposed to the surface paint. Sometimes, the yellow dye was printed in a grid over white-resist areas to create an alternating white and yellow motif on an indigo ground. Indigo was also printed with a shockingly bright green, which created a slightly raised surface print. Indigo was used for plaids and homespun fabrics as well as wool, which was dyed in skeins (known as yarn dyeing) before being woven. Highly glazed woolen fabrics are found in quilts, often in indigo blue.

Most of the indigo from this period is dark, almost black, sometimes with a purplish cast to it. Some indigo-blue prints have pale blue designs. Besides the deep rich indigo color, a dark blue known as Prussian blue or Lafayette blue was used. Another blue, a pleasant robin's egg shade, was printed on only one surface. It was sometimes used as a ground color behind floral motifs in chintz prints.

Yellows, from soft pastel through brilliant sunshine to mustard, were available. Many natural plant dyes, together with various mordants, produced several different yellows. These plant dyes were made from fustic, weld, quercitron, onion skins, nut shells, and bark, among others.

Yellow was used as an accent color in multicolored prints. A yellow, brown, and green color scheme, known as drab, was popular around 1800 and was used in large fabric prints (roller prints) for furnishings. A yellow, brown, and red combination, another favorite color scheme, was used in pillar prints and other large chintz prints. A yellow ground with small black, brown, or red motifs was also fairly common.

Yellow was used in combination with various blues to create different shades of green. Fabric yardage was printed with blue or yellow and then overdyed with the other color to create various shades of green. Green as a one-step printing or dyeing process was not developed until 1809, and two-step printing for green was used continuously until the 1900s.

Purple dyes were derived from logwood, lichens, seashells, or madder, and any one of these choices could be fugitive (unstable). This problem continued until the 1930s despite many attempts to overcome the difficulty. Occasionally, a strong purple color will appear in antique quilts and fabrics, but take extreme care if you want to preserve the color. Purple dyes can be damaged by sunlight or humidity, usually fading to a nice soft brown.

Turkey red was a common and dependable dye with a long history. It was made from the madder plant and has been used since ancient times for solids and prints. It was sometimes combined with a chrome-yellow raised overprint, similar to that used with indigo. After 1812, a Turkey red ground with a chrome-yellow overprint was also likely to have additional colors, including blue, green, or black. Large-scale stylized paisley prints were common, as well as small-repeat motifs. Other dye stuffs that would render red were fustic, barwood, logwood, and redwood, as well as cochineal, a dye made from the Kermes shield louse.

Pink, often a lighter shade of madder red, was popular. These were soft dainty pinks, frequently created with a small, closely spaced pattern of red on white to create the illusion of pink. Stylized swirls and flowers in shades of pink were fairly common. Sometimes deep intense pinks were used to create highlights in red florals. Dark rose colors also frequently occurred. Some evidence in older quilts suggests that many pinks were not colorfast. Patterning in other colors on large floral prints indicates a loss of pink, and some tan flowers were originally pink and a trace of the original color can be seen hidden in the seams.

Browns were popular and easily obtained from many natural sources, such as walnut hulls, clay, madder, onion skins, and wood chips (butternut, walnut, and other woods). Combinations of minerals also produced brown and black dyes.

If you see a deep brown with a warm tone, it could be a manganese dye. This dye was sometimes used for printing a ground color on floral prints, and it may be "tendering" or showing damage from the dye and the mordants (setting agents). Unfortunately, many dark brown dyes have proved fugitive and have bled into other fabrics or have seriously damaged the cloth. It is fairly common to see an old quilt in which the floral motif remains quilted to the batting and backing, but the dark brown ground has crumbled away.

Soft browns, which now look slightly dusty, were also available. A light tan or sand color was in use, both as a solid and as a print ground. Glazed chintzes were often brownish pink (derived from madder). They remind one of old sepia photographs.

Blacks were made by combining several different dye colors to create richness and depth. Logwood, sumac, birch, oak, and iron were some of the ingredients used to make black dyes. Sometimes, tree galls were used, or fireplace ashes were added to the pot. Black dyes were also guilty of tendering, and it is not unusual to find a perfectly wonderful early red or yellow fabric in which all the little black parts have disappeared, leaving tiny holes. Elijah Bemiss (*The Dyers*

Companion, Dover, reprinted 1971) was already aware of the problems with caustic dyes for creating black, and cautioned dyers of this fact in 1812 and 1815.

FABRIC PRINT STYLES

The fabrics that have survived from this time suggest that highly glazed or polished surfaces were desirable. True, we are seeing mostly the best fabrics to be had, which were often preserved in fine quilts. It appears that textiles that received rough handling and frequent washing, such as heavy woolens, linens, and homespun, have lost their glaze. Cotton fabrics were usually made with fine strands of yarn and were closely woven and smooth to the touch. Linen was commonly used as a backing for quilts. Many woolens appear in quilts from this time, often in a solid color. Sometimes the woolens were printed and glazed. Few examples of woolen fabrics in yard goods are available from this period.

Some fabrics had closely packed overall prints, which were the design source of modern-day calicos. Other designs included trailing vines, trees, florals, simple geometrics, and fill patterns such as small, stylized florals. Because simple geometric designs were easy to produce, they were fairly common.

In contrast to the small overall prints, whole panels were printed with one large vase of flowers or stylized tree design for use in bedding or scarves. Coordinating borders were also printed. Large-scale pillar prints, featuring Greek or Roman columns, with swags of ribbons and florals, were common in the 1780s through the 1830s. Prints which featured ribbons, bouquets, and swags were also popular. Pictorial *toiles de Jouy*-style fabrics, featuring events of the period or classical literature themes, appear in fabrics of this era as well. Larger-scale prints may have been used for furniture, including drapes for the windows or bedstead, or for wallcoverings. Whole suites of furniture were designed with coordinated chair cushions, draperies, and wallcoverings.

Many fabrics included some kind of background fill print in lines or dots. They were printed with tiny nails or metal strips mounted into wood blocks, but near the end of the 1700s, most of these fill patterns were being produced with copper rollers. These finely printed designs, known as mill engravings, are distinctive. Vermiculate patterns (squiggly lines), picotage (tiny pin dots overall or clustered to create shading), and ornate grid-work were often used as ground prints with larger floral or pictorial patterns. A cartouche, a scroll-like ornamental frame, was a favored element in fabric prints. These fabrics were sometimes printed with alternating floral stripes and with drastic changes of flower size in the same print.

Neatly spaced identical floral motifs were reminiscent of the prints from India. While these fabrics may truly be from India, the style was so popular that it was copied by practically every print house in Europe. The copies were known as Indiennes. The same can be said of prints with quaint fanciful motifs that imitate Oriental designs. These prints, borrowed from Chinese motifs, are referred to as Chinoserie. Also during this period, Etrusien and Pompeian prints were being made, as well as French Provincial fabrics.

Some prints from this period may appear to be finely drawn, with delicate vines, fine picotage, or vermiculate patterns. Others may appear to be crude and simplistic in design, with the prints registered improperly. Colors may be precisely placed, printed in a blob, or hand painted, as evidenced by drips or a misstroke of the brush.

QUILT STYLES

Styles that were popular included glazed-wool calamanco in large sections (whole cloth), Tree of Life quilts (printed whole or made from appliquéd cut-out chintz), broderie perse, and medallion styles, which had more than one pieced or appliquéd border. Pieced blocks set on point with printed alternate blocks were also popular. Quilts made in the "strippie" style, consisting of rows of pieced blocks alternated with strips of fabric, were also common. Pieced block patterns that were popular for alternate sets, strippie quilts, and borders on medallions included eight-pointed stars, Bethlehem stars, sunbursts, mosaics (hexagons), Nine Patches, four patches, and squares on point. You will rarely see appliquéd borders, but those you can find may be made from cut-out chintz, sawtooth designs, or floral and leaf motifs. Wide chintz borders were common.

Quilting was often done in an overall pattern, featuring swags, Everlasting Tree, or grids of squares or diamonds. Many quilting design elements relied heavily on straight-line patterns, though feathers, clamshells, and leaf patterns were also used in American quilts. Quilting patterns for this period rarely contained "by-the-piece" quilting. Whole-cloth quilts relied heavily on feather and botanical motifs. Some quilted petticoats were recycled as whole-cloth quilts.

Larger quilts (94–120 inches) were commonly made. A bed from this time, often the main furnishing in a household, might be so large that it held an entire family within the cozy draped bedstead. The large quilts, covering the entire bed, draped almost to the floor to keep out drafts. Sometimes, a trundle bed was hidden underneath, and a quilt might be made large enough to accommodate the trundle.

It is not uncommon to find quilts that have two corners cut out at one end. These quilts were adapted for four-poster or tester beds (a four-poster with a canopy). With the cutouts, the quilt lies flat at the corners. Borders on these quilts were usually designed so that the pattern continued around the end of the bed.

Occasionally, one may see a quilt with silk or wool crewel embroidery, though it is more commonly found on unquilted spreads. An occasional stencilled quilt or spread may also be found, but these are even more rare. Silk quilts were more common in Europe than in America in this time period.

Fringes, tassels, or other fancy edge treatments occur occasionally on spreads or quilts of this period. The quilts that have survived through the past 200 years have been fine treasured family heirlooms, and these were often finished with a flourish. Fringes often do not survive the years intact, however.

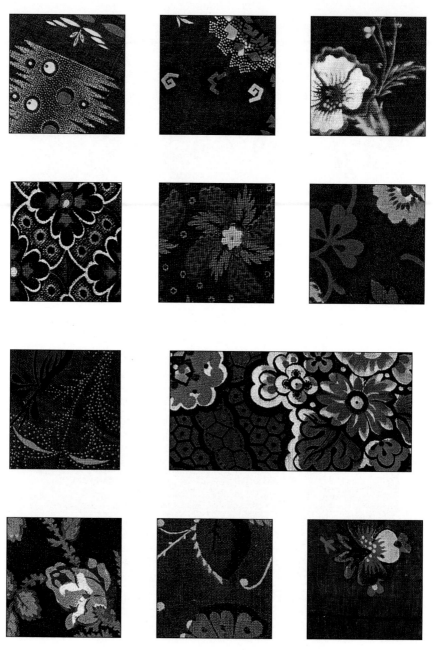

Brown ground with bright floral prints.

Brown ground with bright floral prints.

Simple pattern, dark browns.

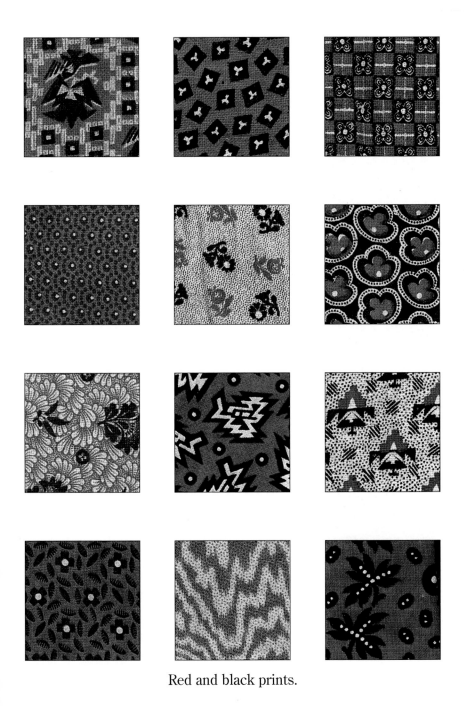

Red and black prints.

Red and brown with black; variety of background fills.

Large-scale chintz.

Turkey red ground with chrome yellow and multicolored prints.

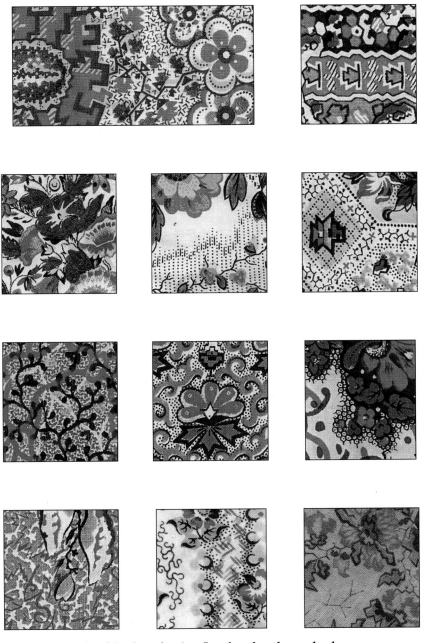

Multicolored print florals, closely packed.

Multicolored prints on light grounds, medium spacing, with picotage.

Multicolored on light ground, wide spacing.

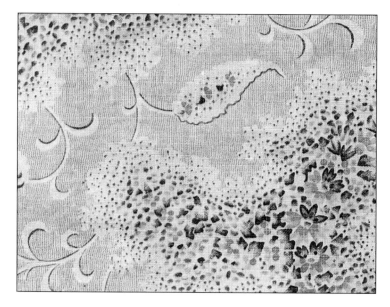

Lace print; tan, blue, pink combination; all scales.

Light grounds, small-scale prints.

Pinks and fugitive pinks.

Rosy browns and fugitive reds.

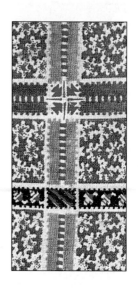

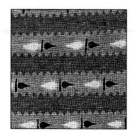

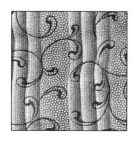
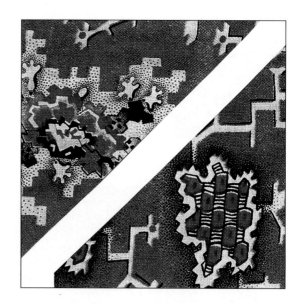

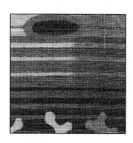

Fugitive purples.

Browns.

Tan, yellow, red combination; orange.

Tan to mustard tones.

Early cheater cloth.

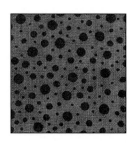

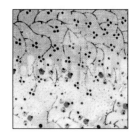

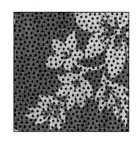

Variety of greens.

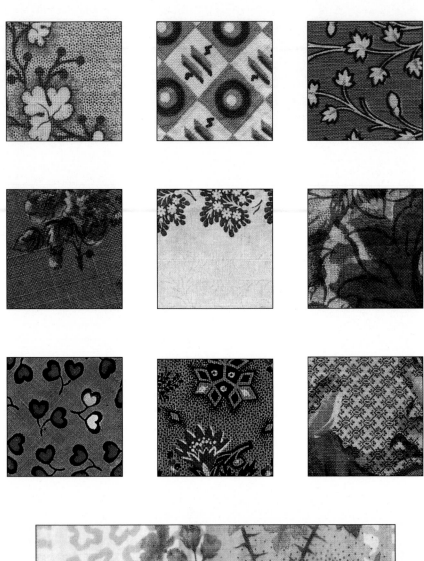

Variety of blues.

Indigo blues with pale blue, white or green, blue toile.

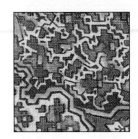

Chintz. Multicolored pale paisleys.

WESTWARD HO!

ABOUT THE PERIOD

This was a time of expansion on the American continent. The colonists had long been established in the East. Some had made the long trek across the continent, and some had sailed around South America. Gold was discovered in the mountains and in California. Fine prairie land, for those interested in farming, was there for the taking, and take they did.

European import fabrics arrived in eastern port cities, influencing the types of prints used there. The imports also influenced the products from American mills. American mills and printworks were running successfully and producing textiles as fast as possible because the population was growing at an astounding rate. Immigrants arrived and fanned out across the continent. Many new states joined the Union. It was a time of great cheer, great hardship, and great promise for the settlers.

Advances were being made in all areas. Between 1832 and 1834, Walter Hunt invented a sewing machine. Thomas Howe invented and patented another type in 1846, and Isaac Singer made one available on the installment plan. Quilts made before the 1830s would not have any machine sewing, with the exception of later repairs. Quilts with machine sewing are unexpected in the 1850s because sewing machines were unavailable to most of the general public until 1856.

In the cultured parts of America and in Europe, schools were being established to provide training for artists and designers. The Royal College of Art, Royal School of Needlework, and the Societé Industrielle de Mulhouse were established in this period.

In 1851, the Great Exhibition took place in London. Textiles and textile production techniques were important features of this grand event, which was held in the Crystal Palace exhibition hall.

TEXTILE COLORS

Many people believe that all old quilts are basically brown. This isn't the case. Fabrics from this era have a wonderful intensity of color that can make your heart beat fast just to look at them. The colors are often used in stunning combinations we might not consider today.

Prussian blue was a popular color with a richness and depth that stand out in quilts of this period. This blue was probably first produced in America in the early 1830s, but was known in Europe previously. Prussian blue was often used to create those lovely fabrics that were graded from light to dark blue and back again, known as rainbow or ombré prints. You will find that this blue was often printed with a light tan figure, perhaps enhanced by a black or white edge. Evidence found in the seams of early quilts indicates that this tan fabric was often originally pink.

Another color combination that appears in quilts of this period is a pale blue print containing stars, pin dots, bird's eyes, or lines with a dark indigo ground. You may have to look twice to see that the small figure is really blue and that your eyes are not playing tricks on you. Pale blue also appears in large floral prints, but only rarely. You can also find deep, dark indigo prints with an overprinting of yellow, impossible to distinguish from earlier periods. Green on indigo blue was still in use during this era, but it was used in higher concentrations to make an even brighter green than in previous times.

Turkey red, which was used for background color, is useful in fabric dating. The fabrics have a white discharged print, which may be partially overdyed with black, bright green, bright clear blue, or yellow. The discharge and dye process was discovered in 1810 and was more popular in the 1850s. Today, the fabric is somewhat sought after. Often, a lovely quilt has been spoiled by the fabric loss caused by the mordant in the black dyes. The yellow may be raised, which would indicate that the piece might have been printed over with a yellow chrome paste, or the yellow may lie smoothly in the pattern, indicating a dye.

Turkey red was not the only red. One brownish red occurs frequently during this time. It was often printed with a dark brown outline and a medium brown and white print. Sometimes it also included coppery brown accent colors. A bright blue accent was sometimes used in this combination. Wide stripes in combination with this reddish brown might also include a pale green shade instead of the white. At the present time, the green may be so faint that it is difficult to discern. When viewed in the proper lighting conditions, the green is usually identifiable. This combination continued through the 1870s.

Pinks can be dark, almost red, shades or soft pastels, featuring floral prints or paisleys. Deep pinks show up in the highly floral pillar prints and their companion fabrics. Pale solids are also found, particularly in Baltimore albums and other appliqué work. Double pinks began to appear in the 1840–1850 quilts. They have a white ground printed closely with a red or pink, then printed with another darker pink or red over that. Often they have a regular pattern of white dots. They are so closely printed that the ground appears pink. Some people call these cinnamon or double pinks. Large-scale pink ginghams were also popular.

Purples from 1840–1860 sometimes appear as a dark print on a white ground or occasionally as a medium solid purple ground with white florals and black outlines, crudely printed. Because the dye was fugitive, it may have turned to brown and not be recognized as purple. Some fine-line prints on white grounds also appeared, mostly in geometric patterns. Purples in combination with brown or red madders were also common. A chemical purple was not developed until 1862.

A brilliant yellow was used as a ground during this period. It usually contained small black, brown, or red prints. This was the yellow accent color most often used in Baltimore album quilts and in quilts from the Pennsylvania region. Small, closely packed yellow prints, which became known as butterscotch, were sometimes used as backgrounds in quilts. These often contain the same patterns as double pinks, double purples, and double blues.

Greens included chartreuse, drab olive green, dusky forest green, and almost aqua. A dark blue-green, printed with blue, dusky yellow, and black, appeared in this period as well. The prints included squiggles, teardrops, or bubble shapes.

A deep yellow green, the most recognizable green, is an overdye, usually printed with a small black figure. The overdyed greens often contain a small yellow figure along with the black ones. This print and dye process was used for a long time. The colors and print shapes are difficult to pin down to a specific date. There are a few prints, made only during this period, that have finely detailed form, often including leaves, seaweed, and bubble shapes. These prints also have more yellow than later versions and were popular in 1850s quilts. They appear often in the best appliquéd red and green quilts.

Fugitive overdyed greens, which may show streaks of yellow or blue, can also be found. Although a single-step green is reputed to have been invented in Jouy, France, by Samuel Widmer in 1809, overdyed greens remained in use in American quilts through at least 1890. A deep cool aqua (penciled) was used in combination with browns in woven fabrics or in some ombré prints. It passed out of use in the late 1850s.

Browns were dependable colors and were used liberally in many prints. Manganese as well as madder and wood extracts were used to dye browns. Black grounds are rarely seen in quilts from this period, but black prints can be found as accents on other colored grounds.

FABRIC PRINT STYLES

The ombré print was a particularly well-known fabric style in 1830–1850. The fabrics were dyed with one color that was graded from light to dark or bright to dull. Some ombré prints were graded from one color to another. The colors included brown, purple, blue, teal, or pink-red. In some ombré fabrics, one color was graded in one direction, and a second color in the opposite direction, down a width of fabric. Ombré fabrics sometimes contained images of lace or leafy floral designs. These wide designs were often combined with a stripe or other element of stark contrast. In appliqué quilts, these fabrics were used to create the illusion of dimension. As you look at ombré fabrics, be aware that, because of the width of the design, pieced quilts often do not show the true character of the fabric used.

Ombré fabrics were also used in fancy silk ribbons and wool challis. As wool challis, this print style continued into the 1860–1870 period in a much narrower width of grading and rarely as cottons, but as ribbons, it was popular until the 1930s.

Wide, simple plaids in weaves or prints, including madras-style weaves, can be found quite often today and are identical in color and style to madras plaids being made today. Wide-stripe prints, with a great degree of variation between one section of the stripe and another, are normal for the time.

Light-colored grounds often have motifs that are about a half-inch in size and laid out in rows or regular patterns. Aqua blue, purple, soft pink, and brown are commonly found printed on light grounds.

Fine ground prints, such as picotage and vermiculate patterns, were used less than in earlier times. Solid grounds were common.

QUILT STYLES

Possibly the most famous style of quilt from this period is the Baltimore album. Almost completely appliquéd, this style features floral wreaths, monuments, ships, people, and animals as common themes. They were often made as presentation gifts for ministers, brides, or others. It was once rumored that these quilts had all been made by one person, Mary Evans, of Baltimore, Maryland. Further research has shown that this is not the case. These quilts are being copied in the 1990s, in abundance, because of the books written about them by Elly Sienkiewicz.

Broderie perse quilts with cutout chintz appliqué and, occasionally, quilts with fine buttonhole-embroidered edges were still being made until the 1860s.

Friendship quilts featuring signatures of friends and family were also known as album quilts, after the fad of collecting signatures in a kind of scrapbook. At the time, many people were leaving the settled Eastern seaboard and traveling west into the unknown. No one knew when or if they would see each other again, so the ladies took a little bit of their friends along in the form of quilt blocks. Usually, the blocks were as individual as the makers. Sometimes, however, the well-wishers used the same pattern in each block. The most common pieced pattern in this style of quilt is the Chimney Sweep or album block, which has a white section in the center useful for signatures.

Red and green appliqué quilts, most often with 9 to 12 blocks, were popular. These quilts frequently included stuffed work in alternate blocks or borders. Many of these pieces were well-planned endeavors because the amount or red and green fabric used was sufficient to complete the entire quilt. These quilts were often designed with stylized or realistic flowers and leaves arranged in sprays, wreaths, or bouquets and placed in urns or baskets. A quiltmaker's best work was often displayed in a red and green appliqué quilt, saved for special guests or to show on a bed. These quilts are now considered collectors items.

Cutwork, in which the appliqué was made like paper snowflakes, was quite popular, and a skilled paper cutter was considered an artist. These appliqué patterns were used for blocks in many album quilts.

A white-work quilt, with hand-tied fringe or hand-made lace, is a special item from this period. This type of quilt is entirely white and quilted and stuffed with extra cotton wadding to create high relief designs in certain areas. They may feature floral elements or pictorial scenes.

Blue and white quilts with alternating blocks, stuffed work, and fringe also seem to have appeared about this time. These quilts most commonly featured stars.

Many of the quilts are heavily quilted, with ornate patterning. Double and triple rows of stitching are fairly common, as well as closely quilted grids or background fills. Feathered wreaths are popular. Pictorial quilting as well as botanical elements are found in open spaces. In white-work quilts, as well as samplers, frequently you can find the name of the maker within the quilting design.

A date or the name of the maker, written in ink or cross-stitch embroidery, may be found. Templates of copper were made with ladies' names and with designs, which might feature something of interest to the maker, such as a musical instrument or floral bouquet. Sometimes, the ink has bled onto or disintegrated the fabrics. Signatures in cross-stitch are rarely found after 1850.

Wreaths, Oak Leaf and Reel, Laurel Leaf, and other stylized floral motifs were popular for appliqué. Piecing patterns still included a preference for eight-pointed stars, Nine-Patch, and Bethlehem stars, as well as album blocks and Mariner's Compass. More piecing patterns and variations began to appear in this period.

Quilts featuring blocks set side by side, sashed or unsashed, take the place of the strippie style, for the most part. Alternate blocks of plain white, especially in red and green or blue and white quilts featuring heavy quilting or stuffed work, were also popular. Additional design elements used in 1830 to 1850 included decorative borders with appliquéd swags or pieced work.

Quilts remained large in size and often included a cutout for a four-poster bed, but not as commonly as in the previous period. Antique quilts made in the area we now know as the Midwest rarely include cutouts, while New England quilts continued the tradition for this time.

Some antique dealers specialize in fabrics from this period, but they are rare and often expensive. Some of the easiest to find examples of these fabrics are in quilts and clothing in museums. Beauties fortunately show up from time to time, because quite a few, in remarkably fine condition, appear unexpectedly in family collections. One New

Hampshire quilt dealer reported finding some early quilt tops that had been used as covers for turn-of-the-century quilts. The makers had quilted or tied the covers, using the newer but worn quilts as batting. These tops had been salvaged from family trunks in the 1930s Depression years.

Cross-stitch date. Light grounds.

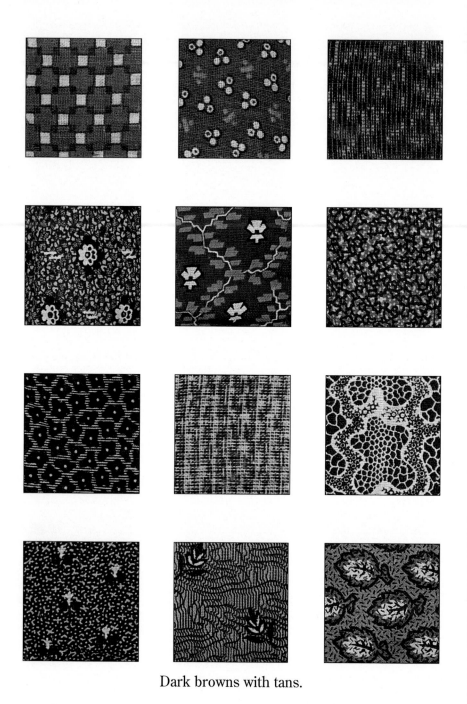

Dark browns with tans.

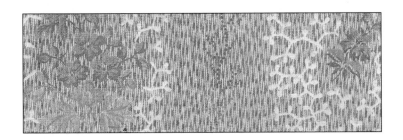

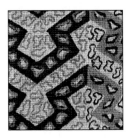  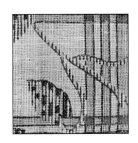

 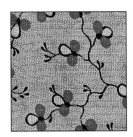 

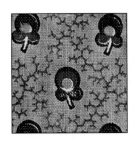 

Tans and taupe.

Tans with red, brown, purples, or blues.

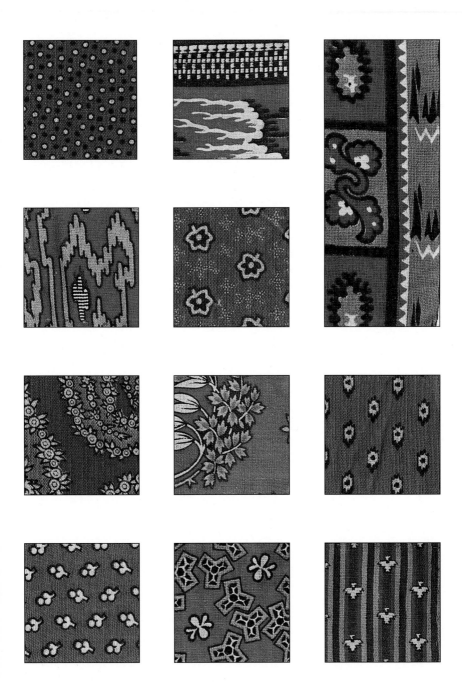

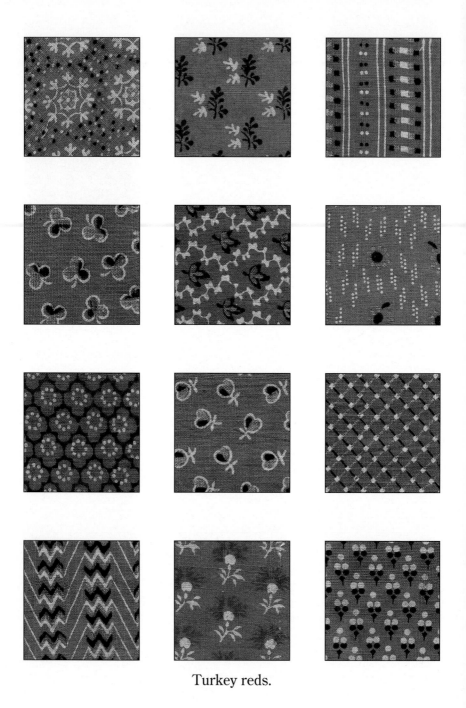

Turkey reds.

Pink varieties.

Strong unfaded purples.

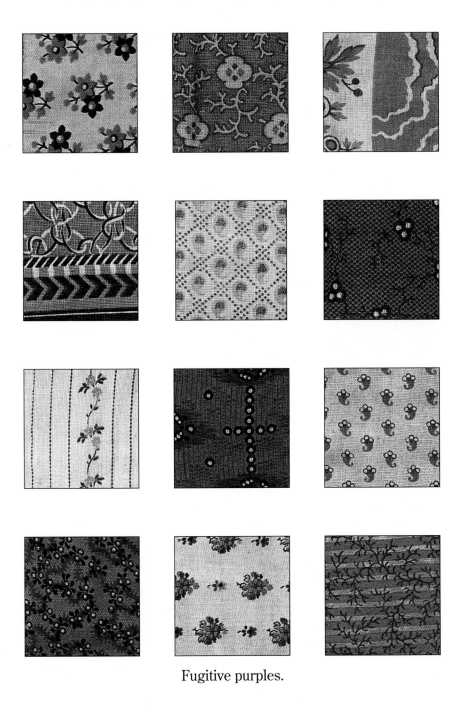

Fugitive purples.

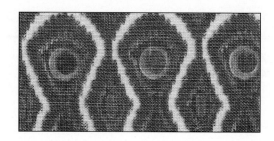

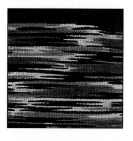
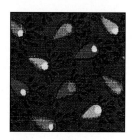

Dark teal green.

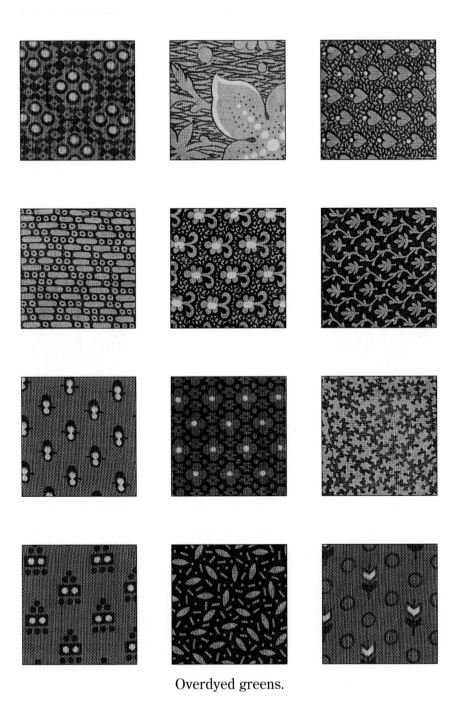

Overdyed greens.

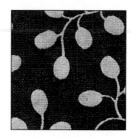

Greens that are not overdyed.

Light blue.

Brilliant blues, some Prussian.

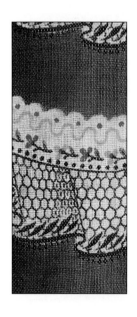

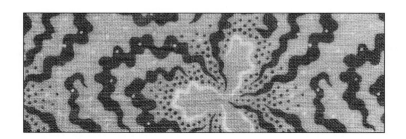

Brilliant blues, some ombré, some fugitive pinks.

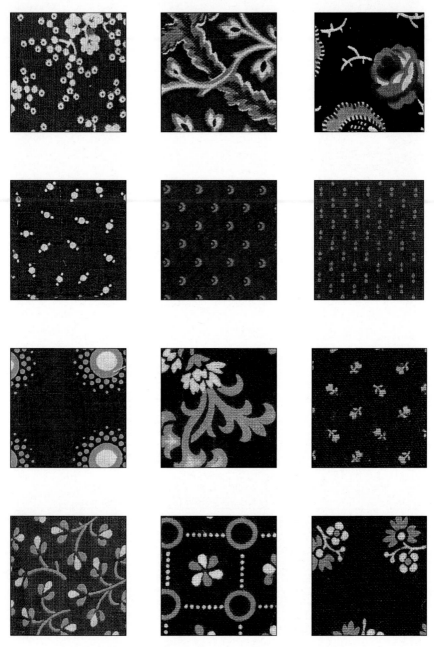

Dark blue and indigos, some with chrome overlay.

Chrome yellows with red, brown or black.

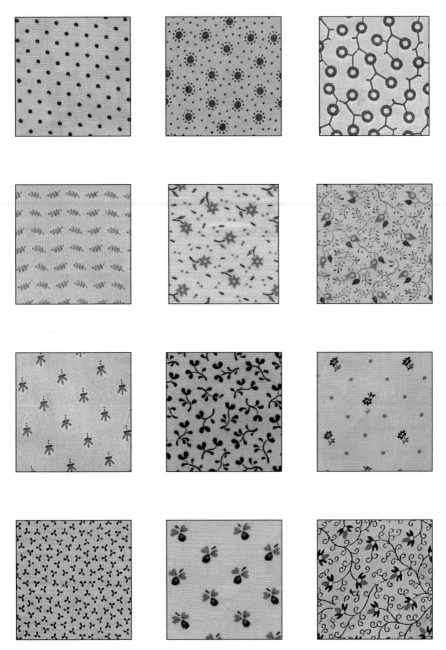

Chrome yellow, small prints.

FIRST CENTENNIAL

ABOUT THE PERIOD

The great historical occurrences of this period include the War Between the States, the nation's recovery from the war, and the assassination of President Abraham Lincoln. Prince Albert of England died in December 1861 and left Queen Victoria, alone and in deep mourning, to rule an empire. America celebrated the first 100 years of government, and everything from clothing to buildings to interior decor was beautifully decorated and even over-decorated.

The Civil War had a great effect on the history of textiles in America, especially because Southern plantations were no longer able to produce the amount of cotton required to supply the country. The northern mills were not purchasing cotton from the South, so as not to provide funds for the Southern war coffers. However, women created usable textiles for the soldiers at an incredible rate. Treasured family heirlooms were hidden to protect them from theft by soldiers, and these included prized quilts. Almost as fast as the women could create quilts, the soldiers had need of them.

In Europe, technological advances were being made in the field of artificial dyes. An accident of chance by William Henry Perkins, a chemist attempting to create an artificial quinine from coal-tar derivatives, produced the first known chemical dye. Many other developments followed, creating other new and colorfast dyes.

Aniline dyes were mentioned in the April 1870 issue of *The Ladies' Friend* magazine, which called them "charming new tints brought out of late in ribbons and dress goods." On the same page, there is a note concerning the recycling of old rags, particularly wool, to use for "flock for wallpaper, padding for mattresses, and Prussian-Blue for the color makers."

The development of the sewing machine was also cause for comment in that publication. To quote: "The sewing machine, like a magician out of fairyland, turns off yards upon yards of flouncing, and ruffling, and fluting, and furbelows generally, and the ladies put them all on, restrained only by their inches in height; so that at present it really seems that nothing was gained by this beneficial invention." The writer continues, "The labor and weariness of the needle are not abated one bit." Incidentally, at the end of the magazine are ads for Grovers and Bakers sewing machines for a price of 55 dollars.

William Morris, an artist and textile designer in London, established his company in 1861. His first designs were based mainly on Gothic or medieval themes. He greatly opposed the use of the new aniline dyes and advocated the natural dye processes and the personal involvement of the artists in their creative works. Others joined in his beliefs and adhered to time-honored traditional crafts, the beginning of the influence of the arts and crafts movement.

TEXTILE COLORS

Madder browns are the most distinctive colors of this period. The overall appearance of this type of dye gives the print a coppery tone. Fabrics dyed with madder often have a mixture of colors in the print, including a warm dark brown, light tan brown, dark Van Dyke brown, and orange. Occasionally, a red or a bright clear blue may also be present. Madder prints were associated with stripes, paisley prints, and printed plaids and checks.

Dark chocolate and cocoa browns were also common. They were often used as grounds with white designs. A warm medium brown was also common. Browns from this time were often printed as decorative grounds in more than one intensity, with geometric or floral elements as the main design, which might have included purple.

Solid or mottled browns were possibly from home dyes. It was part of almost every woman's recipe book to have some tried-and-true home dyeing recipes, telling how much bark or how many weeds to gather of a specific kind, and everything needed to make a color. Butternut and walnut were some of the trees useful for dyeing. Often, home-dyed sacking was used for the back of a quilt.

Double (cinnamon) pinks were popular in this period and were often used in brown and pink quilts. These were bright reddish pink with a fine picotage (dot) or with fine lines to produce a light pink ground. They were then printed with a more concentrated area of the same dark pink. A regular pattern of white dots was often included. Prints identical in pattern to the double pinks may be found in golden yellow, purples (possibly faded to brown with age), and double blues, sometimes referred to as Lancaster or Pennsylvania blues. Double-pink prints were made unchanged until the 1920s and are presently making a comeback in reproduction fabrics.

Soft pinks with swirls and a large expanse of white, or regimented patterning of pink motifs with a variety of shades in them, occur occasionally. These fabrics often have widely spaced patterns with buti (squared-off) paisley elements. Ginghams in checks and prints were also popular.

A solid Turkey red was common. The dye was derived from madder, like most of the warm coppery browns. It was often used in fine appliqué quilts in combination with solid greens. Prints similar to the Turkey red, yellow, blue, green, and black combination of the 1850s were still available. The patterns from this time were much simpler, and the fabric was used less frequently than in the earlier versions. Late in this period, and particularly the following one, another bright red appeared. It was after the advent of a new dye, alizarin crimson, and the subsequent demise of the madder-growing industry.

Orange also appeared and may be known as antimony or chrome orange. A deep orange is sometimes now referred to as cheddar by present-day collectors. Women could make this dye on their own from chemicals available at the druggist's shop, but the dye was highly toxic because it contained chromate of lead as a main ingredient. This orange was common in Pennsylvania quilts and was used as an accent color in appliqué quilts. Sometimes this color was guilty of crocking (rubbing off onto other colors). Presently, the chrome orange may be a mottled brownish-green, which usually washes out. Varying the mordant and the quantities of chemicals created a bright yellow.

Indigo print designs changed little over the years from 1830 to 1900. Indigo blue was often dark and deep. Being a vat dye, this blue saturates the fabric and can be seen at the same intensity on both sides. Higher quality, closer-woven indigo fabrics with a clean, crisp print are more likely to have come from the 1860–1870 period. The pattern sometimes appears less distinct on earlier fabrics, and cloth had a tendency to decline in quality toward the 1900s. Some patterns in indigo are still being printed in parts of Africa and Europe. These fabrics are identical to those printed 100 to 150 years ago.

Indigo blue designs were sometimes overprinted with a yellow that had a slightly raised surface. The pattern, sometimes printed in wide swaths of decorative design, may be very intricate. While the white prints can be seen faintly on the back, yellow is less likely to be visible on the wrong side.

There is a clear, bright blue from this period that is found in madder prints, as well as by itself. It was used on a light gray, taupe, or tan ground and occurred as a small print or stripe. Because it was a printed color, it is only visible from the top of the fabric. Bright blue prints were sometimes used on a white ground as floral sprigs. This color was used as a double-blue print. It is thought to have been made only in Pennsylvania, providing the nickname, Lancaster blue, and it is common in the quilts from that area, as are double pinks. It is similar to the double pink – a darker blue was printed over a paler version of the same blue. These blues often turn to a gray-blue when exposed to liquids.

A light aqua appears occasionally, usually printed with another color, like a gray or light brown. It is an unexpected accent mixed with the warm shades of brown and red. This color was also used alone on white grounds, often as a floral sprig.

Purples from this period were often fugitive, turning a brown shade closely resembling the other browns of the time. However, some of the purples have retained their color remarkably well. These prints often have a fairly complicated overall print as a ground, with geometric motifs, straight lines, or zigzag lines. Some prints are sharply demarcated by black and white.

Intense purples and mauves are not commonly found in cotton fabrics of this period, but they were used to dye silks and woolens. As such, they were used in quilts of this period quite frequently.

Many of the greens were also fugitive. Overdyed greens were still in use. The fabric was dyed either yellow or blue and then dyed again with the other color to make green. These green fabrics can sometimes be affected by light or water. Blue or yellow streaks or splotching are an indication of an overdyed fabric. Some of the yellowish greens that we presently see may have been much darker. When in prime condition, the color is the same as that of the overdyed greens from the 1850s but often with simpler patterns.

A pale peach is often quite distinctive in quilts from the 1860–1880 period. This color was used as a ground for floral sprigs or as small buds, often in combination with a pale mint or aqua green.

Red, blue, black, purple, and brown were used in shirting. These same colors were used for printing small floral sprigs or leaf clusters, commonly found as light fabrics in quilts. Red and black, and blue and black are common combinations.

FABRIC PRINT STYLES

Stripes and plaids were fashionable, particularly after Queen Victoria had her portrait painted wearing her ancestral Scottish Tartans.

Selective cutting of these designs could enhance a lady's tiny (heavily corseted) waist, and the cut of her gown.

Paisley prints in all sizes were staples during these years. Large motifs were printed in madder on cotton. Woolen shawls and table scarves were often printed in black or red with bright yellows, blues, and red.

Shirting prints on a white ground were in evidence. Object or conversation prints were also available in 1860–1880 fabrics. Bugs, anchors, horseshoes, and sewing implements were common themes. They were usually larger and spaced farther apart than their turn-of-the-century counterparts, and they were spaced at regular intervals. During the 1860–1880 period, there was a tendency to print these motifs all facing the same direction, in stiffly regimented rows, with more than one color in the print. In the 1880–1910 period, these motifs were more often tossed (unregimented) and printed in one color.

Multicolored sprigs of leaves and flowers on pale grounds were also featured prints from this time.

Fabrics printed to look like textures of something else were quite popular. Chenille, lace, beads, ruffles, ribbons, basket weaves, and moire cottons were all possibilities. Some cheater-cloth prints were also produced.

Fabrics that celebrated the United States Centennial were also popular. Themes included cannons, bells, eagles, and waving flags. The likenesses of historical political figures were printed on commemorative panels. These Centennial prints were often made in madder with red and blue accents or with one color on a white or cream ground.

Fabrics in the quilts of 1860–1880 were not limited to cottons, by any means. Striped silks and brocades were available, as well as woven woolens. Wools were printed with the same designs as the cottons, and optical-illusion geometrics and paisley shawls were popular. Wool and silk prints show up in many quilts from this time, particularly in Log Cabin or Hexagon piecing. Protein fibers, such as wool or silk, absorb dyes more readily than cotton, and the colors are often far more intense than their cotton counterparts.

QUILT STYLES

Quilts from this period are known to have a lot of geometric piecing with not too many fancy curves. Birds in Air, Wild Goose Chase, Log Cabin, and other rather straightforward patterns were popular. Mariner's Compass and other designs along these lines are occasionally seen. More patterns became available during this time, which were distributed through ladies' magazines, often with a minimum of instruction.

Album quilts with multitudes of different appliqué blocks became less popular, and quilts having blocks of a single pattern, straight set or with sashing, took precedence over ones with alternate plain blocks. Alternate blocks, when used in combination with pieced blocks, were often cut from a dark print fabric. Wide borders were still of great importance in appliquéd quilts.

Large quilts still predominated in the eastern states, but quilts became smaller near the end of the century. The batting was usually thin, with a great deal of quilting, particularly with double-rodded or triple-rodded decorative lines. Quilting thread matched either the appliqué or the ground.

Indigo and white quilts became quite popular, a holdover from the ones made in the 1850s. Red and white pieced quilts also increased in popularity. Often, these were made in geometric piecing with an all-over set, or they had pieced sashing. Decorative pieced or appliquéd borders were often added to finish pieced two-color quilts.

Appliquéd quilts were usually red and green with orange, yellow, or pink accents but without the stuffing and trapunto work seen in the 1850s. Occasionally, a quilt may show up with blue leaves. It is difficult to ascertain if the quilt was made with blue leaves or if an unstable green dye was used.

Quilting designs, usually sewn with white or black thread, were often not as complex as those of the 1850s. Thread that coordinated with the appliqué was sometimes used. Machine quilting, which began to appear in the 1860s and 1870s, was usually extensive, and the batting was thin. Echo quilting, similar to that found on Hawaiian quilts, was one of the patterns used for machine quilting. Machine-quilted quilts from the 1860s and 1870s are more likely to have have been made of appliquéd blocks. Often, the appliqué work was done by machine. The machine-quilted blocks were often set together and then bound on the back with slip stitching or fabric strips, similar to the quilt-as-you-go method of the 1970s.

Pieced pillow cases from this period are an unexpected treasure. These are most often attributed to Pennsylvania, though some are found far from there. Sometimes there was a quilt to match, though the pillowcases and quilt may have been separated sometime in the intervening years.

Madder-dyed, copper-toned, 1876 cheater cloth.

Stripes, plaids, paisleys in copper-toned madders.

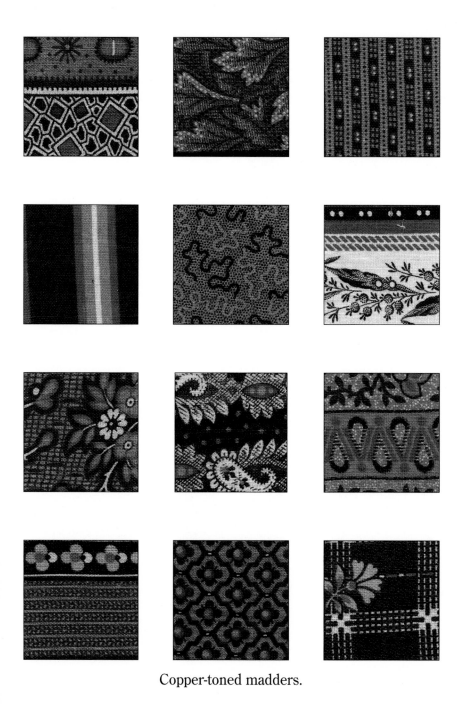

Copper-toned madders.

Madder browns.

Cool browns.

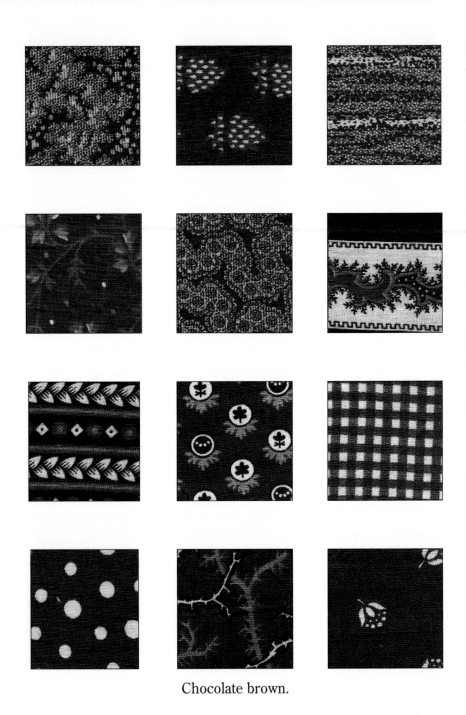

Chocolate brown.

Muted browns, some with accent colors.

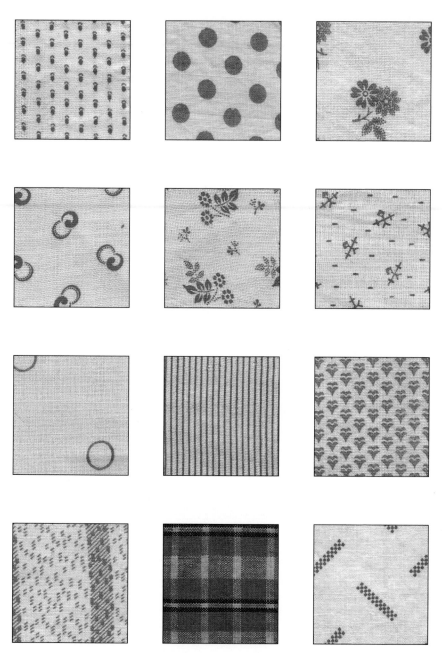

White ground with red figures.

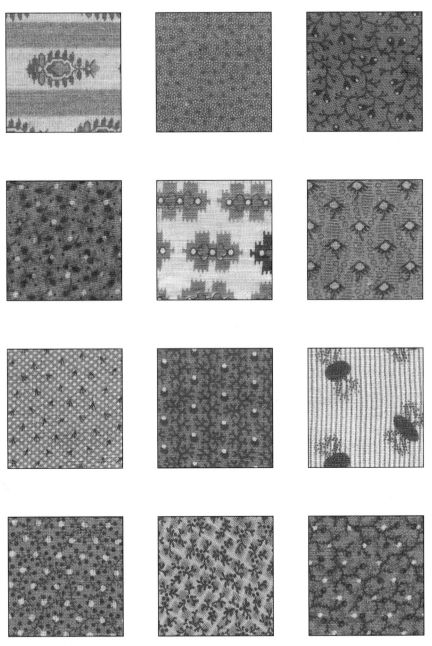

Double pinks or cinnamon pinks.

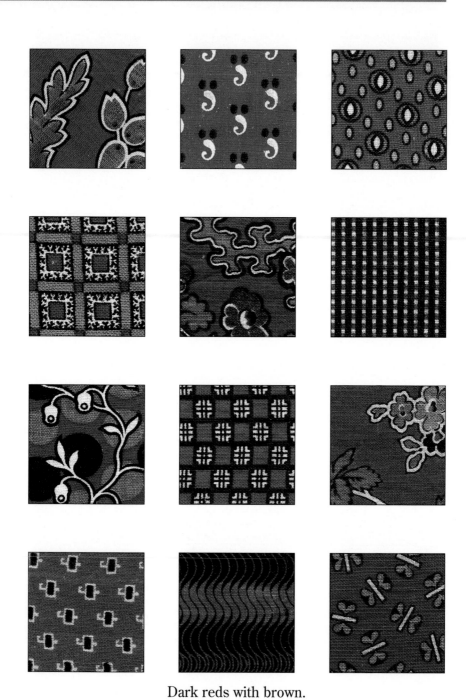

Dark reds with brown.

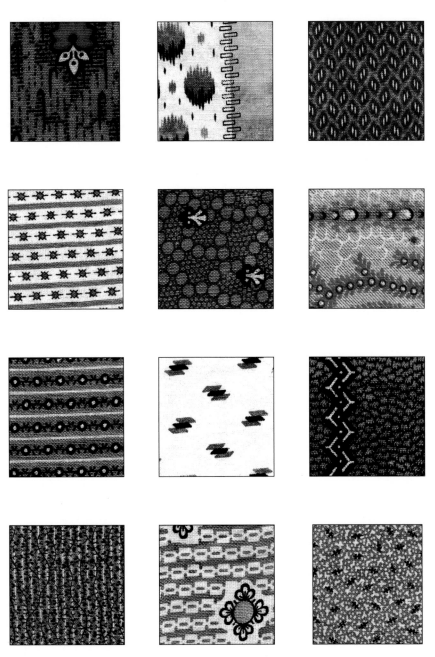

Purples (fugitive dye) faded to browns.

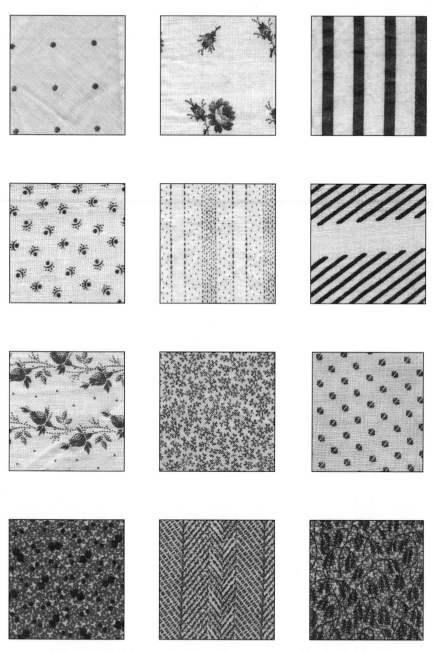

White with blue grounds and Lancaster (double) blue.

Gray-blue tones with browns or grays.

Dark grays and indigos.

Minty greens on light grounds, overdyed greens.

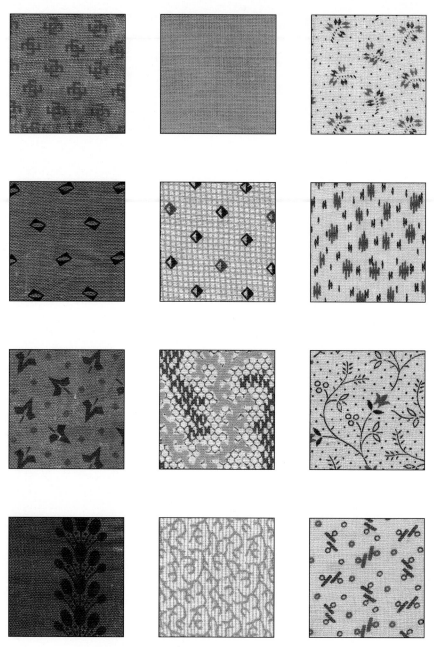

Tan, cheddar, butterscotch, and chrome yellow.

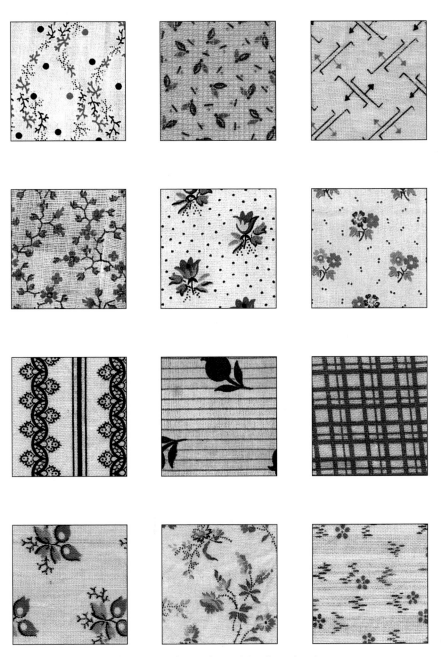

Light grounds with multicolored prints.

Wool challis.

TURN OF THE CENTURY

ABOUT THE PERIOD

Dark, somber colors typify the years between 1880 and 1910. The mourning of the Empress Eugénie, for her husband, Napoleon III, and Queen Victoria for her husband, Albert, and her mother, the Duchess of Alba, is thought to have been a major cause of the shift to darker fabrics. Strict adherence to mourning rites were practiced in those days, which included wearing black clothing for the first year after the death of a family member. After that, one might wear gray, dark purple, or dark blue.

The World Exposition in Philadelphia in 1876 had a profound effect on the types of fabrics available and on design styles, as did expos hosted by Japan in 1862 and 1876. The Japanese exhibits featured the types of designs for which the country subsequently became famous. Japanese style was formal and asymmetrical, whereas Europeans were used to seeing formal but symmetrical patterns.

The arts and crafts movement, late in the century, had an influence on home furnishings and fabric manufacturing as well. A few stylized florals began to appear late in this period in sharp contrast to the dark fabrics from the early years of this era.

Women and men found their world changing around them. During the mid-1800s and into the early 1900s, women were encouraged to be the caretakers of home, husband, and family. Fancy work was an accepted pastime. At the end of the century, suffragettes encouraged women to take an active part in deciding who would govern them by protesting for a woman's right to vote. Women were encouraged to speak out about their preferences and to take an active part in activities outside their homes. Better education for women became a more important issue.

TEXTILE COLORS

The 1897 Sears Roebuck catalog offered a variety of fabric styles and colors. Shirting prints came in black, red, blue, pink, or brown. Mulhouse Percales were described in the catalog as having "dainty little figures" in pink on white, black on white, or blue on white. Also listed were percales in light blue, medium blue, or pink. Wash dress goods were sold in light blue, pink, old rose, and lavender. Linen lawn was sold in navy, light blue, and tan. Minerva Percales had it all. They were offered in "white, light blue, yellow, linen, or pink ground, small, medium and large figures, plain and fancy, wide and narrow, straight and serpentine, tape and hairline stripes" as well as "new, neat scroll designs: also a nice assortment of checks, stripes, anchors, horseshoes, etc...."

Some sateens were listed in the 1897 Sears catalog. They included floral prints, in natural flower colors, on black. White on black was also available. A few colors were offered in sateens: light, medium, and dark tan; pinks; cardinal red; scarlet; light blue; navy; and medium blue.

Mourning prints were listed as a specific category in the 1897 catalog. An entire department was devoted to black dress goods and another to silks. All-black prints and silver prints were also listed and were considered suitable for mourning.

The 1902 Sears catalog offered a selection of fabric choices with many illustrations. New colors appeared, such as heliotrope, plum, garnet, and violet. Dutch indigo was still commonly found in the catalog. Black prints with red highlights were referred to as Garibaldi prints. Oxblood was a term found in the 1902 Sears catalog which had not been used in any of the catalogs mentioned previously.

Butler's wholesale catalog (a dry-goods supplier in Chicago) in 1903 listed some of the fabrics commonly found in this period. The ground colors offered were black, navy, indigo, cadet blue, cardinal red, Turkey red, burgundy, crushed strawberry pink, or lavender.

In the 1908 Sears catalog, there were listings of chambray in various colors, not limited to the soft pale blue we are familiar with from the 1990s. There were pink, light blue, dark red, navy, cadet, Nile green, tan, dark brown, and steel grey.

Sateens were also manufactured in more color choices in 1908, including pink, light blue, Nile green, myrtle green, primrose yellow, tan, champagne, medium brown, royal blue, navy, Turkey red, dark cardinal, slate, cream white, pure white, and black.

Percales were made in navy, cadet, black, or wine. Percale shirtings offered white grounds with red, blue, or black motifs. Mourning prints were not mentioned in the reprint of the 1908 catalog.

Some of the bright reds have faded to salmon pink, orange, or brown. This coloration is evident in some of the quilts made across the southern tier of the United States, where the fabrics may have been dyed with Georgia or Arkansas red clay. Also, some fugitive madder reds, for which water was used instead of the oil required for a true Turkey red, turned a dusky reddish brown.

There is a subtle difference between the red tones from the early 1860s and those from the later years of 1880–1900. While the earlier deep red color was derived from madder plants through a long process, the particularly bright red from the latter half of the century might have been the chemical dye, alizarin, also known to artists as the basis for crimson.

Indigo blue prints were referred to in all the Sears catalogs as Dutch blue or German blue after countries known for the skill of their blue dyers. Some of the exact patterns are still being produced with the original techniques. With indigo's distinctive odor, the fabrics even smell the same. Indigo, that ancient dependable dye, received some competition from a new blue dye at the turn of the century. Synthetic indigo, like mauvine and alizarin, was derived from coal tar. If the same techniques are used for creating the patterns, synthetic indigo is almost indistinguishable from the original.

Cadet blue (a misty blue) was often printed in combination with black or white. It is a distinctive color for this period because it was not used before 1880. It was vat dyed, similar to indigo, and was therefore equally blue on both sides of the fabric. Cadet blue fabrics may have a resist print design in white, which leaves a smooth surface. Other cadet blue prints may have been printed with a white paste, which creates a raised pattern, usually also white. Occasionally, they were printed with a small pink or red accent, though this occurs more often after 1900. The early 1900s brought a clear blue color, used in solids and prints, what many people now refer to as "baby blue."

Also printed at this time was a combination of reds, soft browns, and pinks used particularly in soft florals, border stripes, and cheater cloth. These fabrics appear to have the same types of prints as those dyed with madder, but faded. They were actually printed with a different dye, possibly cutch (Oriental acacia). It is fugitive when wet and may stain other fabrics, or the print can have a fuzzy outline because the dye bled. This fabric is often fragile.

Black fabrics in wool, silk, or cotton were common. This was the period of the Gibson Girl with white shirtwaists, black drop-front skirts and hair piled high on the head. Black cotton sateens were often printed with floral sprigs, some in white and some in colors.

Black grounds with white discharged (bleached out) prints were popular and were usually listed as mourning prints. Also, an occasional black with a white resist was printed with a delicate pattern of yellow on the surface. This print is rare and appears only in this time. It is similar to the yellow-over-indigo prints of the earlier periods, but with a black ground. Other black prints with brilliant surface designs provided a great relief from the somberness of mourning prints. Fabrics were printed with hot pink, chartreuse, electric blue, purple, or yellow, exotic colors for the period. The overprint appears almost neon against the black, and it can be felt on the surface of the fabric, just like the yellow overprints.

Brown was used but in much smaller quantities after 1900 than in the early part of this era. These browns were generally softer, and they were used in fabrics similar to mourning prints. Browns were more likely to be used in weaves and as prints on light grounds than as backgrounds. Black and brown prints are notorious for disintegrating.

Claret or burgundy prints with white resist were common. The wine color was available in wools in the 1860s and became popular in the 1880s in cotton. This color continued into the early 1920s as a vat-dyed color with white sprigs, lacy effects, or geometrics. The pattern was sometimes formed by a white or chrome-yellow overprint, which sits on the surface. Sometimes, small black figures were used. Some of these wine-colored fabrics are not colorfast when wet.

Purple and green dyes were often fugitive and may have washed away or faded to brown. Germany owned the patent for a stable green, but the green dyes made in America and used in American quilts were often unstable. Dark forest greens, commonly used with white, were somewhat more dependable and colorfast. Medium-greens and purples were often used together in madras-style plaids and checks.

Yellow print fabrics were available, most often as small calico-style prints. Chrome orange and cheddar from this time were often used as solid colors. They were sometimes used extensively in a quilt, sometimes sparingly as an accent color. Orange was particularly effective as a contrast to indigo blue or black. Orange was a color rarely used for clothing.

FABRIC PRINT STYLES

Shirting prints are usually thought of as typical of this era, though this type of print was actually common throughout the 1800s. Shirting prints were manufactured with a white or cream ground printed with small geometric figures or stripes. During this period, the figures were usually printed in only one color, such as black, blue, red, pink, brown, or green. Stripes or geometric motifs were common.

Many other cotton prints from this period were made with a dark ground and a white discharge or resist print design, giving most quilts an overall dark color. This coloration existed until 1910–1920, when white or lighter grounds with colored prints became the norm.

Checks, stripes, pin dots, polka dots, lace print stripes, floral sprays, and scrolls were mentioned in the catalogs. Damask was a standard table covering, which came in either white or Turkey red. Damask was used occasionally in quilts.

Furnishing fabrics were often used for quilt linings, including twill weaves, good for heavy wear, or cretonne, which was a thin smooth fabric. Either of these types were printed with large, multi-colored florals.

Homespun-type fabrics had been popular in previous periods, but during the 1880–1910 years, they were extremely common. Ginghams, checks, houndstooth, plaids, and stripes reminiscent of ticking or farmers overalls were advertised in each of the catalogs previously mentioned. Apron checks and plaids often found their way onto the backs of quilts and pieced blocks. Checks and stripes were often found on heavier cloth than the period prints. Fabric was dyed in the yarn stage to make checks, plaids, and stripes. Mordant damage often occurred to the colored yarns, leaving spaced weaves like Aida (cross-stitch) cloth.

True homespun fabrics are impossible to differentiate from factory-made cloth. In some regions of the country, homespun was made with a great deal of skill until the late 1930s. Some factories provided cloth of lesser quality.

Fine shimmering silk or mercerized cotton threads were often woven into stripes and plaids during this time. These fabrics were used for ladies' dresses as well as men's shirts. Usually containing a white ground, these decorative thread weaves often included a simple print, usually black. Madras plaids also had thick mercerized threads woven into them in a decorative pattern. This feature was especially prevalent at this time.

Cotton prints of this era were notorious for being thin, like cheese-cloth. They often had a lower thread count or finer threads than we are used to in the 1990s. These thin fabrics wore out sooner than the heavier cottons and pulled out at the seams more readily. Ladies' magazines of the time advocated making narrower seam allowances to remove excess weight from quilts. The combination of poor cloth and narrower seam allowances was a disaster for many of the quilts from this period.

Cotton flannels were striped or plain, or they had large paisleys in the design. They were commonly made in pale pinks and blues, but dark burgundy, red, black, and browns also existed, particularly in the paisleys. Flannel cigar and cigarette premiums began to be distributed at this time.

Silks from the 1880–1900 period were also made as cheaply as possible in many cases. Light silks were weighted with mineral salts or gall dyeing to make them move like heavier, more expensive silks and to rustle, which was a much desired quality in a silk gown. The colors were usually rich jewel tones, though silk brocades and jacquards were printed in any color. Machine-embroidered silk ribbons were available, as well as silk bengaline (a heavily ribbed weave), grosgrain, and picot-edged ribbons. Silk fake furs were added as trim on clothing and were used for piecing in crazy quilts. Commemorative ribbons were given away at conventions, and silk pictorial squares were given away as cigarette premiums.

Cotton sateen, the poor man's silk, also made its way into turn-of-the-century quilts. Easier to care for than silk, sateens were washable and came in a variety of colors.

Wool fabrics were woven in simple to complex patterns, but rarely in the bright print wool challis known in the 1860–1870 period. Men's suiting often contained strands of a different thread color, usually gray or blue, to add visual interest. Sometimes suiting was woven with two or more thread colors. Utility quilts were made from these fabrics, and the style of weave has not changed much from then to now.

QUILT STYLES

Quilts from 1880–1910 were often dark overall. Because the predominant colors were black, dark blue, deep red, brown, and claret, the quilts were usually quite subdued. Utility quilts were often patterned with simple geometrics, large-scale blocks, and wide sashings. Some of the more common block patterns were Bow Tie, Bear Paw, Nine Patch, four patch, 15 patch, Thousand Pyramids, hexagons, and all-over squares. There was a temporary fad of collecting fabrics for one-patch quilt designs in which no two fabrics were alike, today referred to as charm quilts.

The quilts from the late 1800s through the early 1900s were more ornate than earlier pieces. It was also the heyday of crazy quilts. These were mostly made of silks of various weaves including, but not exclusively, brocades, jacquards, velvets, bengalines, and commemorative ribbons. Cigar bands, felted flags, corduroy, fake furs, cottons, and wools were sometimes incorporated.

Crazy quilts are known for being encrusted with botanical and zoological embroideries, as well as initials and dates. Some also have needlepoint portraits, three-dimensional floral appliqué, silk ribbon or chenille embroidery, or hand-painted botanicals. In other words, if it didn't move, the ladies were likely to stitch it down to one of their fancy coverlets. These quilts were heavy, and the fancy encrusted ones were preserved mostly for show. Cotton or wool crazy quilts were mostly made to be used.

Ornate crazy quilts largely fell out of favor before 1915. They were time-consuming to make and required a wide variety of fabrics. Occasionally, a later highly decorated crazy quilt may be found, but as a general rule, the intricate embroidery required for a classic crazy quilt is lacking in these later varieties. There has been a resurgence of crazy quilts and embellishing in the 1990s, however, complete with embroidery, beading, and ribbons.

Other quilts were made from silk, such as the Log Cabin or silk "puff" quilts. Antique silk quilts are usually fragile and require extreme care in handling.

Wool quilts are of particular note in these years. Beginning in this period, the Amish and Mennonites of Pennsylvania and Ohio made highly graphic wool quilts in solid saturated colors. Other quilters of the time made quilts from wool suiting and dress scraps. Tailors' or salesmen's samples in rectangular shapes were commonly used for piecing, but crazy patch wool, embroidered with crewel or pearl cotton, was a standard style as well. These heavy quilts were often lined with flannel. These comforts, or suggans, as they are sometimes called, were often tied with warp string or wool yarn, making the top and lining easy to remove from the batting for cleaning. Sometimes another worn quilt was used as the filler.

Quilts containing wools and flannels were common from this time through the 1950s. Since woolen suiting has changed little over the years, these are difficult to date using the woolens alone. Dates can be determined from the print fabrics used in conjunction with the woolens, but this method is not always accurate.

Crazy quilts and Log Cabin quilts, styles which utilize a foundation fabric for piecing, were often only bound or lined with a print fabric or silk and then tied. It was common for the ties to be visible on the back but not the front. These types of quilts were also used without lining or binding.

Few appliqué quilts have been attributed to 1890–1910. Those that exist usually follow the standard color scheme of red and green with pink or orange accents. These quilts are usually smaller than their earlier counterparts, and they often lack the quantities of decorative border elements so admired in earlier quilts. The greens have a tendency to turn brown, and other dyes may have faded to white. Appliqué "ghost" quilts that have white elements on white grounds are not uncommon, indicating fugitive dyes. The quilting thread often matches the element that has been quilted.

For quilting during this period, simple quilt patterns were often used that were fast and easy, and often a dark thread was used. The stitching may not have been extremely even because of the common usage of thick battings. Great sweeping arcs were sometimes quilted over the entire surface of a quilt, and this type of pattern was known as elbow quilting, or Baptist or Methodist fan (presumably determined by which church you attended). When fans started at either side, leaving a narrow unquilted strip down the middle, the quilting was sometimes referred to as a razorback. For quilts with thin battings, a simple twist or cable was often incorporated. Double or triple rows of quilting with a decorative pattern were sometimes used. The quilting stitches often crossed seam lines as if they did not exist. After 1900, it became popular to quilt blocks and borders with diagonal or diamond fill patterns, in contrast to the earlier overall quilting patterns. Quilting with a heavy string or warp yarn was not unknown.

Battings from this period could be purchased from a store, ordered from a catalog, or hand carded at home. Home-grown, cleaned, and carded battings were sometimes thick and wadded or could be extremely thin and even. Many quiltmakers were skilled at carding and preparing thin battings. Some were very serious about having clean cotton, and some were perhaps in a hurry and not quite so particular. Wool battings were available, most commonly in the northeastern states and the Rocky Mountain region. However, the most common batting material was cotton, which was available and used all over the United States and its territories.

Non-shirting light prints.

Black and white.

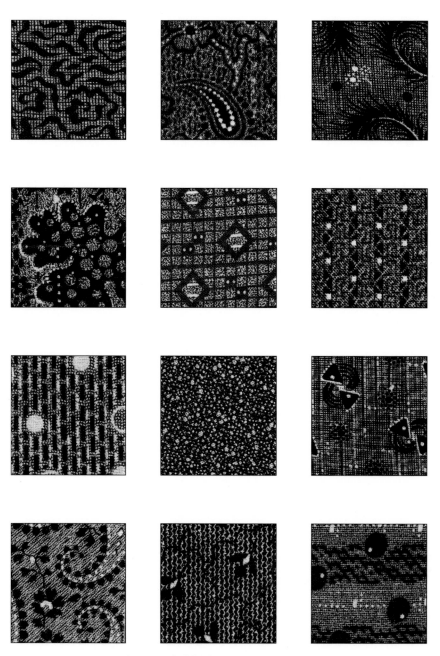

White with black mourning prints.

Black with bright textured overlays.

Dating Fabrics: A Color Guide 1800–1960

Black with bright textured overlays.

Indigo and white.

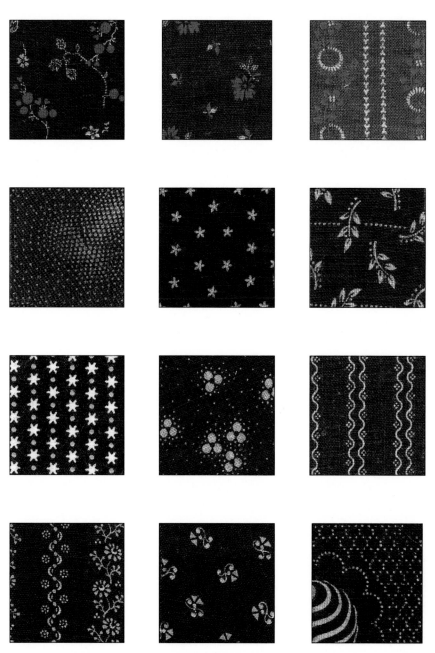

Indigo or cadet with red, pink or chrome yellow.

Cadet blue and white.

Blue weaves.

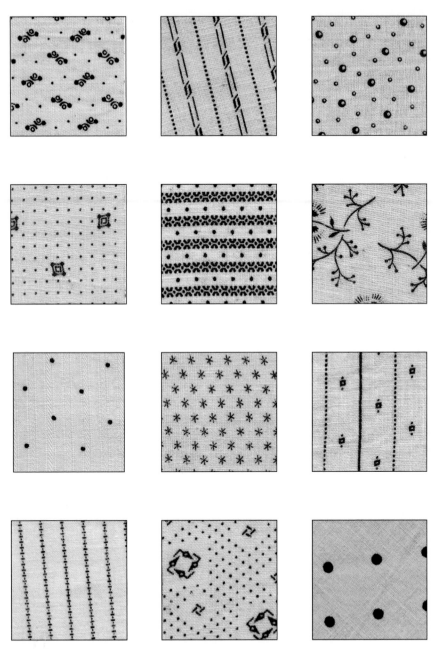

White ground shirtings with black motifs.

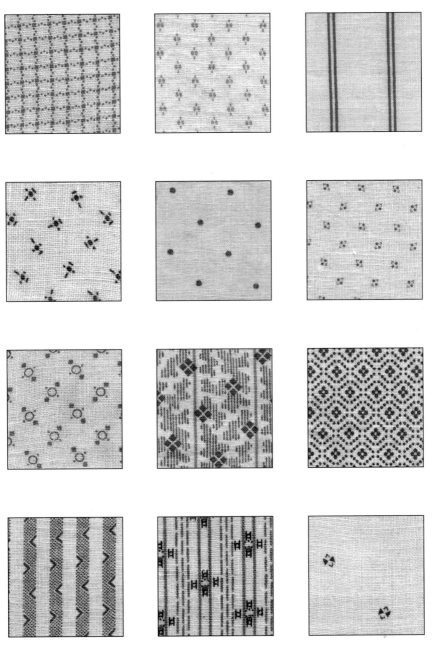

Shirtings with various color prints.

Variety of browns.

Brown weaves.

Variety of greens.

Green weaves, yellows, chrome orange.

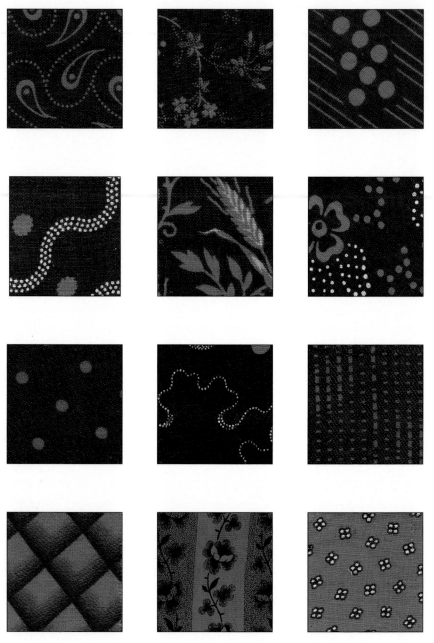

Black with red print, some possibly Gerabaldi prints.

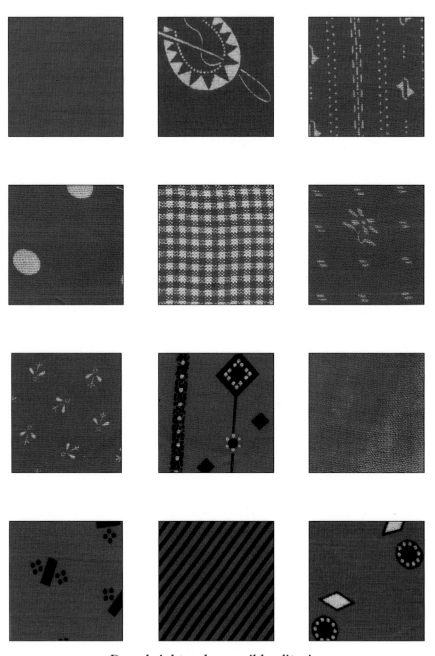

Deep bright reds, possibly alizarin.

Burgundy or cranberry reds with white resists.

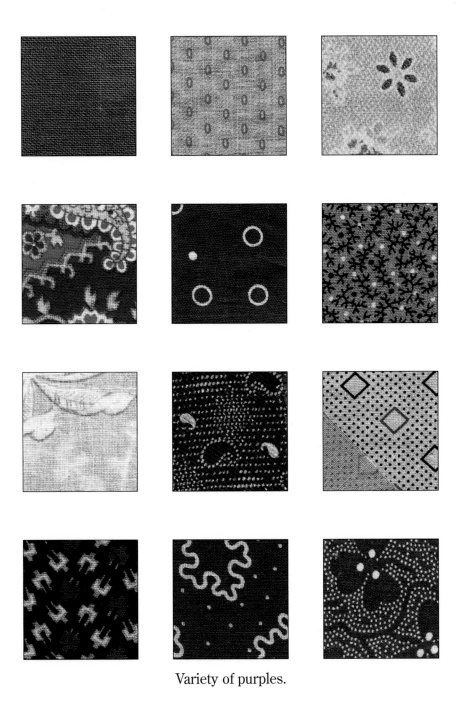

Variety of purples.

Salmon pinks and faded reds.

Cinnamon pinks or double pinks. Ginghams, printed or woven.

Large scale floral.

Dark brown with pink.

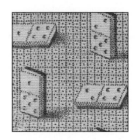

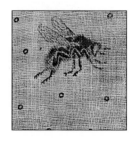

Conversation prints, large overprint paisley

Cigarette silks.

Cigar felt.

ROARING '20s

ABOUT THE PERIOD

World War I took place. Women won the right to vote and the right to do many other previously forbidden things. There was more available to do outside the home during leisure hours. Inside the home, a movement in decor, reminding people of their Colonial or Early American roots, inspired a renewed interest in quiltmaking. However, the quilts women attempted to duplicate were those of only 50 to 70 years before rather than colonial quilts.

Art Nouveau designs were used in many places of business and homes. This influence can be seen in the print designs on fabrics of this period and in the types of designs developed for quilt patterns.

The years between 1910 and 1925 were transition years, with a gradual shift from the darks of pre-1900 through the pastels of the 1920s to the clear bright colors of the 1930s.

Historians theorize that fabric colors may have lightened because of the passing of Queen Victoria, who had been in deep mourning for many years after the death of her husband and her mother. The queen had made it fashionable to be a widow. Many Civil War widows were also passing away. In addition, it may have been an economic move on the part of manufacturers, because pastels could be manufactured with the same dyes used in smaller quantities. Many new dyes were invented and became popular during this period. Gone were the muddy colors of the 1900s.

TEXTILE COLORS

The use of some black and white prints continued into the 1920s, though in crisper, more Art Deco styles. Black and white geometric prints, like squares and circles, are distinctive of this period. Black and white prints from this era usually have a white ground with a black print, whereas the black and white prints from the previous era most often featured a black ground with a white resist or bleached print. The heavy, overpowering all-black prints were nearly gone, though occasional holdovers from the scrap bag appear.

From 1900 through the 1920s, a distinctive color was used, a red with a slightly bluish overtone. It was often used in combination with white for embroidered blocks featuring flowers, children, or animals. It was often the "dark spot" on an otherwise pastel quilt. After the mid-1920s, this color gradually gave way to a new red tone that was more brilliant and had an orange overcast. The new color was used in solids and prints, and the other darker color was phased out.

Pinks started to get a lot of attention at this time. Dusty rose was especially popular. Double pinks were still in use, indistinguishable from 1860s varieties most of the time. Double-pink print ginghams were still common. Gingham check weaves and prints in a pale to bright pink of any size imaginable were popular. Reproduction calico prints were made, duplicating early larger-scale floral pinks from the 1820s and the double pinks of the 1860s. Be aware that the pink dyes were sometimes fugitive, leaving a "ghost" white area with a faint pink in the seam allowances. Pink was common in flannels.

The use of burgundy with a white figure decreased and almost came to a halt. With the early vat-dyed burgundy prints from 1880 to 1915, the back of the fabric is mostly burgundy with a faint white print showing through from the front. For fabrics made after 1930, the back is mostly white, and the colored print seems to sit on the front's surface.

A soft, clear sky blue appeared at this time. It is most noticeable in juvenile prints featuring cartoon designs, such as airplanes, toys, small barnyard animals, and children, usually from the early 1920s. A brighter clear blue was much used in diaper prints (overall small geometric designs). Light blue chambray was used much more often in this period than any other, but chambray was also manufactured in navy, pink, red, brown, or green. A fugitive blue is also apparent in some quilts, leaving a ghost-white area.

A bright yellow appeared in weaves and prints, commonly in conjunction with black or brown. This color continued through the 1930s in prints, though usually in a larger scale. Yarn-dyed woven fabrics in this two-color scheme possibly indicate a 1910–1925 date, while an additional color indicates a date closer to 1930 or later, and it is more likely to be a print.

Pale melon colors appeared, also in woven fabrics or prints. A true orange became more popular in the late 1920s for grounds or accents.

A lavender purple is easiest to find in woven designs, but an occasional print shows up. Purple prints are more common than before. Many purples from this period are fugitive, though bright, clear colors do appear in the 1920s. These dyes became far more dependable in the early 1930s in both solids and in prints.

In the greens, woven fabrics were the most dependable for color-fastness, but constant improvements were being made in dyes. Mint greens, which retained color relatively well, were becoming possible. By the late 1920s to the early 1930s, green was becoming a trustworthy color, with only occasional fugitive dyes.

FABRIC STYLES

Fabrics from the 1900–1915 period were often thin, light, and semi-transparent. The general quality of cloth improved during the 1920s, and the fabrics used in quilts were often of a fine weave and evenly packed. Much of the fabric from this period, when found in its original state, has a light sheen of finishing glaze on it. In the 1930s, printed feed sacking became popular, and one can find an almost even distribution between smooth, even-weave fabrics, and coarsely woven, thick-threaded fabrics in the feed sacks as well as fabric on the bolt.

Special decorative-effect weaves and homespun-type fabrics are found in quilts from this period. The word "type" is used because it is almost impossible to differentiate between true homespun and factory manufactured "homespun." The Marshall Field's fall catalog of 1916–1917 introduced silk fancy plaids, which have a cotton base with silk threads running through in a pattern, highlighting specific areas with a shine. These were called "a new and novel idea," though earlier quilts show evidence of these types of fabrics. Coarse white cotton cord was used in a similar manner. In addition, there were many newly designed fancy weaves in a wide array of colors. Some of these woven designs were referred to in dry-goods catalogs as Red Cross stripes.

Edwardian ladies took to the new fashion consisting of all-white batiste and piqué dresses with fancy pintucking and lace inserts. Many women wore heavily beaded dresses for evening and special occasion wear, which tended toward lighter-weight fabrics, such as silk organza, silk crepe, and silk jersey. These dress silks were sometimes used in quilts, but it was thin and poor for quiltmaking. Silk fabrics may suffer discoloration, and black and white prints seem especially susceptible to damage. Some baby quilts were made of silk organza and silk crepe, though few survive. Rayon, sometimes referred to as art silk or poor man's silk, became common in quilts of this period. Linen was used in some quilts, and it is one of the first areas of a quilt to show wear. Any of these fabrics may have been used in quilts of this period, but they often have not survived the wear and tear of age because they are so fragile. When washed, these fabrics may shred.

Common print styles featured squares, lines, circles, or flower and vine prints. Stylized leaf and flower shapes and line drawing prints were common. Prints from the 1920s often featured background patterning, such as crosshatching, pin dots, fine wavy lines, or other fill patterns. In the 1930s, this design style became much less frequent. In the late 1910s and early 1920s, fabric prints often contained only one or two colors with simple geometric patterning or stylized floral images. Art Nouveau had a great influence on the types of prints being made. Cartoon-like juvenile prints were also popular. Prints from this era can be remembered as "spots and rings and cutesy things," because the prints featured bubbles and balloon shapes, as well as chickens in hats and the like.

Fabrics from the late 1910s and early 1920s were also more likely to have been printed in pastel or dusky tones rather than in bright intense colors, the exception being deep red, bright blue, and clear yellow.

In the late 1920s and early 1930s, the tendency was toward brighter and more intense colors. An increase in the number of colors per print is evident. Prints normally included color schemes composed of opposites on the color wheel. These combinations might include orange and blue, purple and orange or yellow gold, and red or pink with green.

QUILT STYLES

Quilts early in this period often contained a simple design of easy to make triangles and squares or large hexagons (three inches on a side). Quilts that included pieced curves were often somewhat simple in design, with patterns such as Robbing Peter to Pay Paul, Drunkard's Path, and Mill Wheel, which lent themselves readily to Art Nouveau two-color-style quilts. It is fairly common to find a two-color quilt from this period in white and black, bright yellow and black, red and black, or red and white.

In the 1920s and 1930s, the three most common designs were the Double Wedding Ring, Dresden Plate, and Grandmother's Flower Garden. Blocks and tops of these patterns were made in abundance, and many were never finished. Fans, Sunbonnet Sue, and other representational patterns of people or things were also popular. The availability of new patterns and designs for quiltmaking reached unbelievable proportions during this period, and discoveries of pattern collections can be made in antique stores and estate sales.

Penny squares, with the design already stamped on, were named because they could be bought for a penny. Young children (and old) practiced their embroidery techniques on these, commonly using Turkey red floss, which was often not colorfast. These squares were used for pillowcases or for quilt panels set with red fabric. Occasionally, the penny squares were embroidered in blue thread and set with a medium blue solid fabric to create a variation of the two-color quilt.

Floral appliqué quilts returned to the quilting repertoire during this era. These were available as kits, which usually featured stylized floral motifs, popularized by the Art Nouveau movement. Kits could be purchased as early as 1912 through ladies' magazine and newspaper advertisements. Often, a bouquet of flowers was featured in the center of the quilt, usually on an expanse of white, in a loose interpretation of the medallion style. Floral elements in the outer edges echoed the elements of the medallion. These quilts have become American classics.

Appliqué quilts that did not come from kits were often made in pink and green or red and green in tried-and-true patterns copied from 1800s heirlooms. Quilters also invented their own patterns, or used available patterns, and incorporated their own fabrics. Unique designs were drawn and created by those with artistic inspiration.

Quilting designs were often as simple as the top piecing. Grids in borders or blocks, separated by the seam line, were relatively common, though fan or rainbow quilting was still frequently used on utility quilts. In contrast to the plain quilting designs, kit quilts adapted floral appliqué motifs to use as part of the quilting design, and they sometimes featured elements such as spiderwebs or feather quilting in the design.

While the 1880–1900 quilt is likely to have black quilting thread, the 1915–1935 quilt is more likely to be quilted with white thread. Some quilts were sewn with thread in a color to match the motif being quilted. It is not unusual to find a flannel lining or other woven homespun-type fabric in a utility quilt, while appliqué quilts and other pieced quilts usually featured a white or solid-color pastel lining.

Many of these period quilts have batting similar to their counterparts from the previous period. Utility quilts frequently contained thick batting (fat, coarse, and wadded), while the fancy decorative quilts had thin batting. A woman in the rural South might still have carded her own batting from home-grown cotton.

Spots and rings and cutesy things, 1910–1925.

Dating Fabrics: A Color Guide 1800–1960

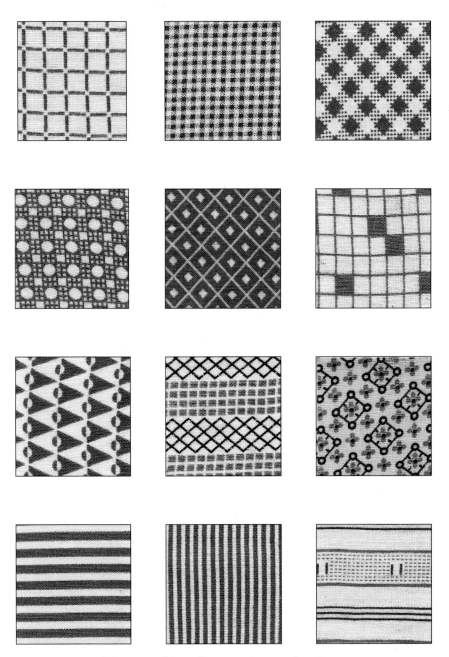

Blue on white, diaper prints and stripes.

Pale blues in a variety of weaves.

Dating Fabrics: A Color Guide 1800–1960

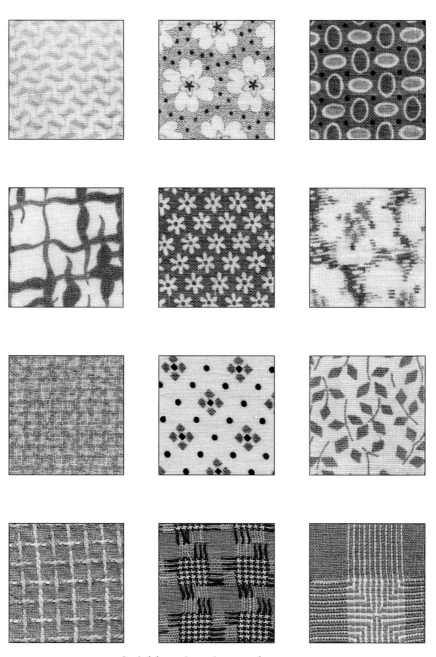

Soft blues in prints and weaves.

Black or gray on white and weaves.

Dating Fabrics: A Color Guide 1800–1960

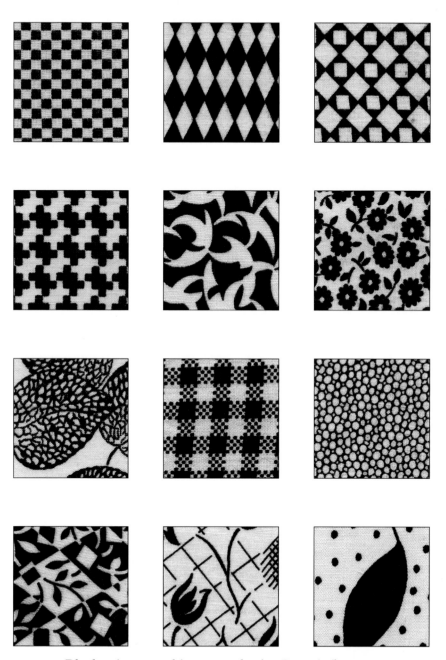

Black prints on white grounds, Art Deco influence.

Black with multicolored prints.

Light browns.

Purple weaves.

Lavenders and purples.

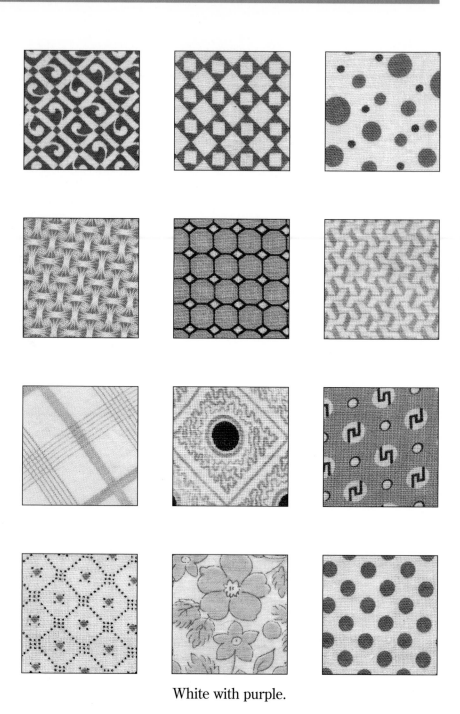

White with purple.

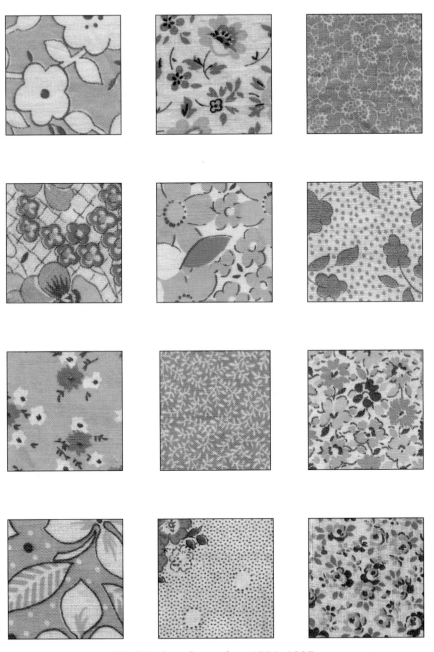

Multicolored purples, 1920–1935.

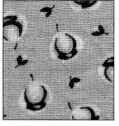

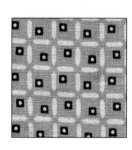

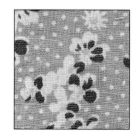
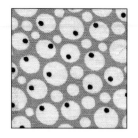
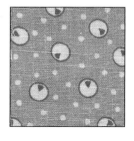

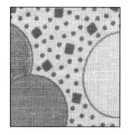

Candy pink, 1910–1920.

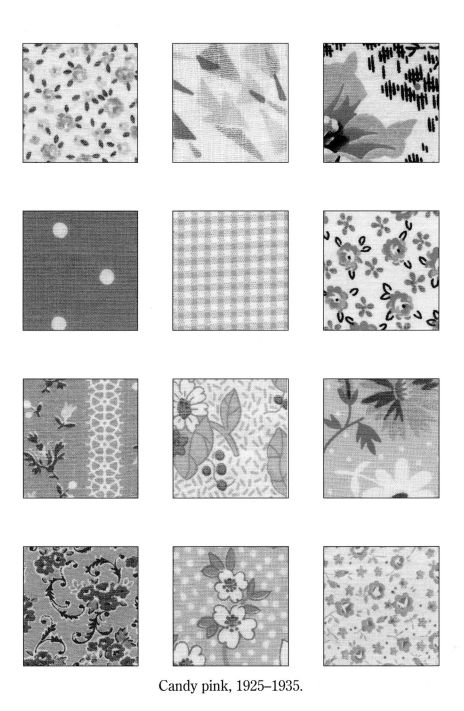

Candy pink, 1925–1935.

Salmon pinks in prints and weaves, 1910–1920.

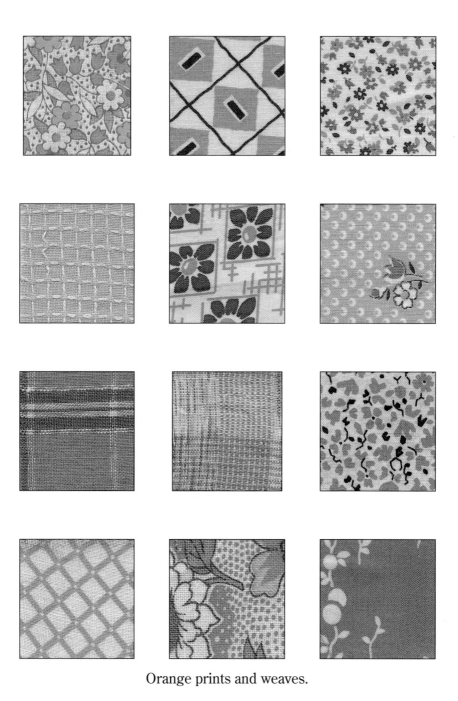

Orange prints and weaves.

Woven reds; Art Deco-influenced red, 1910–1920.

Red and white, 1910–1925.

Red and multicolored prints.

Yellow in weaves or prints.

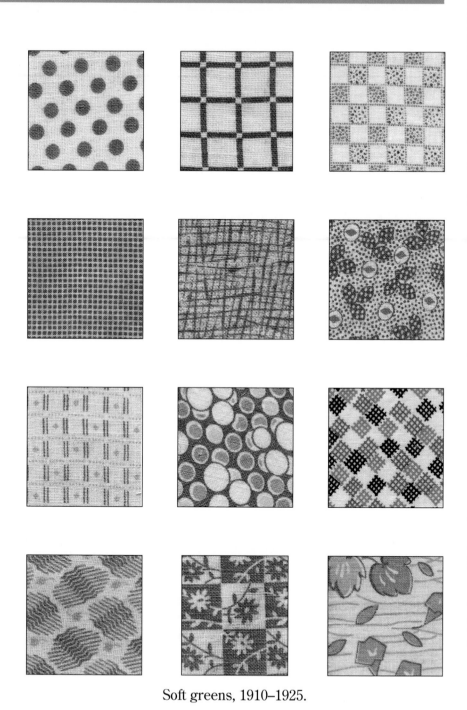

Soft greens, 1910–1925.

Green wovens and prints, 1910–1925.

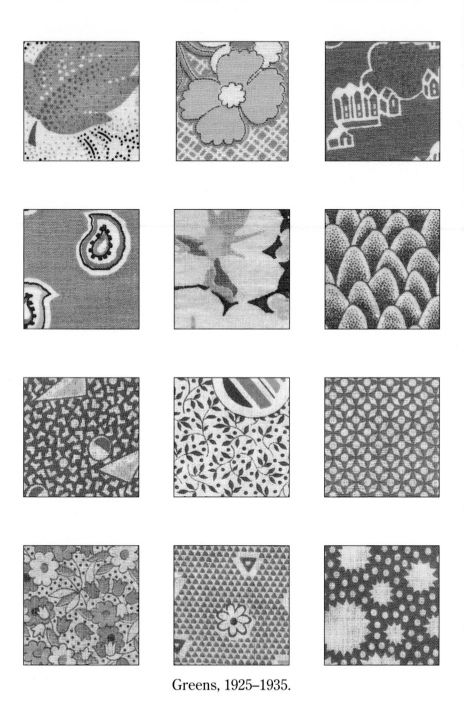

Greens, 1925–1935.

A selection of typical solids.

DEPRESSION ERA AND WWII

ABOUT THE PERIOD

This period in American history takes us from the Great Depression, the Dust Bowl years, and the Second World War, through the Korean War, and almost to American involvement in Vietnam. It was a time of change, of great scientific achievement, medical advances, and the struggle toward flight in space.

When the stock market crashed in 1929, men and women were without work all across the nation. There was little money in most households, and an air of despair invaded many. Women had to make do with what was at hand. The words of wisdom for the day were: "Use up, wear out, make do, or do without."

Salvageable portions of clothing were recycled into quilts. Scraps from dressmaking factories were available by the pound, and these were sometimes used in quilts. Someone's brilliant merchandising idea of using printed fabric for sacking chicken feed, flour, and sugar encouraged women to purchase one brand over another.

Quiltmaking swept the nation during the years between the wars. Great competitions were scheduled, and monetary prizes were offered. The World's Fair Century of Progress competition in 1933 offered a grand prize of $1,000, plus $25 for regional winners. Particularly during these lean years, a few extra dollars in prize money for a quilt could help a family considerably. Advertisements for patterns and kits suggested that selling handmade quilts could make money. Quilts were often made on a barter system in which two quilts were made with one person providing the fabrics and another person supplying the work. Then each party kept one of the quilts.

Inventiveness was encouraged, and newspapers carried regular columns devoted to quilting patterns and other forms of needlework and homemaking. Some of the most famous patterns are those from the *Kansas City Star*. Other newspapers had syndicated columns as well. Patterns by such well-known names as Laura Wheeler, Ruby McKim, Nancy Cabot, and Ann Orr, and booklets by Grandmother Clarke were easily obtained. These were not always names of real people. Sometimes, they represented an organization, which had a multitude of designers, both skilled and unskilled.

During the Depression years, quilts were made in response to the frugal times, and during the war years and rationing, women were asked to make scrap quilts for their own use and leave the blanket supply "for the boys over there." As a consequence, after the war, women in the 1940s and 1950s thought negatively of quilts. If you could buy a blanket as opposed to a quilt, you did, because quilts were made by and for poor folks. Women of the 1940s and 1950s were also too busy raising their families and trying to find their places in a quickly changing world. Often, they had not learned from their mothers the needlework skills needed to make quilts.

To escape the realities of a life of want, Hollywood movies chose to depict lives of splendor, complete with heavy satin dresses and gowns. Bedrooms on the big screen were also decked out in such fabrics. Popular films gave rise to a style of quilts and decor featuring cotton sateen, satins, and silks.

Many women went to work during the wars and frequently did not return to their roles as housewives who spent their days in the stereotypical life of cleaning house, cooking supper, and doing hand-work. Unfortunately, handwork of all kinds lost its importance, and skills deteriorated during these years. This lack of skill shows in many of the quilts and quilt tops of this period.

TEXTILE COLORS

One of the distinguishing features of this time is the common use of bright, clear, multicolored prints. Solid-colored fabrics were used in quantities, sometimes in combination with a multicolored print that coordinated with the solid fabric, but often only solids were used together. Rarely do you find a print with just one color. In fabrics from this time, it appears that someone went wild with the color wheel and decided that any color should be printed in combination with its complement in every colorway available on a white or neutral ground.

The greens of the 1930s and 1940s are distinctive. Nile green or mint green, along with a rose pink presently referred to as bubble gum, are indicative of a 1930s quilt. These two colors were used in combination for thousands of appliquéd quilts with a white or off-white ground. Cotton sateen quilts were often made in pink and green, though other colors were also used. Dark green, in a deeper version of the mint or sage family of the 1930s, was popular in the 1940s and 1950s. It was often used as a solid, in combination with red, in sashing or background piecing.

Military styles influenced some of the olive green shades used during this period, but by no means were colors limited to this palette. Intense bright green, as well as yellow greens and chartreuse, were common in the 1950s.

A most notable addition to the choices of color prints was a bright turquoise, especially in combination with medium or dark blue. The turquoise was used more in 1950 than in 1940.

Navy blue was just coming into its own as the 1940s and 1950s progressed. Red and white were the norm for color accents. Dark blues, always classic, were acceptable for ladies' street dresses. Navy blue fabrics with polka dots in any size were available. Most navy blue was printed, so it does not show on the backs of fabrics except for minor seepage. The exceptions were navy blue gingham, some polka dots, some stripes, and solid-colored fabrics.

Pastel blues were not as common as in the 1930s, having been replaced by medium and dark blue.

Yellows were more golden, particularly when used in combination with brown. Lemon yellow was also apparent, as was a darker color closer to canary yellow. Brighter, clearer yellows and oranges were used in the 1950s. Oranges can be found in soft melon to tangerine.

A great variety of pinks was possible in fabrics of this period, from pale delicate powder pinks to deep dark rose. Toward the end of the era, pinks tended toward brighter and brighter colors, culminating in the hot pink of the 1960s. Used most often in combination with green, pink was also found with blue or in a mixed palette with other pastels. Pink gingham even-weave fabrics were still popular, a favorite since the early 1800s. Deep rose pink used in florals with turquoise or green was common.

Purple frequently appeared as lilac or lavender. Yellow gold with lavender was a common color scheme in prints and quilts. During this period, dark purples were also used almost as frequently as lavender. Two or more purples were favored in the pansy quilts of the 1950s. In addition, prints that featured dark purple, red, and golden yellow with black accents were made.

Red, black, and white combination prints became fashionable, perhaps influenced by the earlier Art Nouveau styles. Reds were either the clear bright chemical red of the 1930s or an imitation of the deep Turkey red of the 1800s. These reds were often used in the appliqué quilts of the 1950s and in the kit quilts that were reproductions of antiques.

Burgundy as a deep-colored print made a comeback in the late 1930s and early 1940s, in combination with a teal green or deep blue and bright yellow accents. This combination continued through the 1950s. These were surface prints as opposed to vat-dyed fabrics.

Browns in combination with yellows or oranges continued in popularity, and usually, several browns were combined in one print. Sometimes, browns and yellows were printed with purples. Neutral colors, such as khaki, were available, though not frequently used in quilts.

Most black grounds were not solid black, and most had a white ground with a black print, such as a crude vermiculate pattern, cross-hatching, or a spotted pattern. Black fabrics often included one high-light color, most often red. There are exceptions to this rule, but it is generally true.

FABRIC PRINT STYLES

As the 1930s and 1940s got into full swing, more colors were added, and the colors became brighter and the prints busier. The prints from this period are marked by the use of two or more colors. Bright colors in contrasting combinations seem to be the rule of the day. Blue with orange; aqua greens with reds; and purples with yellow gold, orange, and green were often used. These colors were all popular in solids as well.

Prints from this era often did not have background fills in the design. The prints were larger in scale, as a general rule, than their 1920s counterparts. A notable technique found in prints of this era is called "grinning" in which haloes were used to separate a motif from the colored ground. This technique enabled textile printers to produce yards of fabric more quickly with less chance of an accidental over-lap of colors.

Stylized florals and circles were popular. Plaids with bands of color about one-half inch wide were common. Wide stripes were popular, too. Checks, plaids, and ginghams in various sizes brought back that "next-door" look to clothing for young women and to shirts for young boys. Polka dots of all sizes on dark grounds, or colors on white, were a mainstay of textile printing. Dotted Swiss and flocking gained in popularity.

Black accents were used as a design feature between 1930 and 1960. Many 1950s prints are almost cartoon-like in the use of black out-lines. Black free-form lines printed on top of colored grounds were also common in furnishing fabrics from the 1950s, following the penchant for amoeba-like shapes in art prints and furniture design. At the end of this period, fabric manufacturers began making gold overlay prints, providing a highlight of metallic sparkle, which was not colorfast. Metallic threads were often woven into cloth to provide sparkle as well.

Feed sacks, always a fabric staple for utility quilts and quilt backings, were manufactured in prints or solid colors and collected or traded to gain certain quantities of cloth. The use of printed or dyed sacking became commonplace during the Depression when fabric was dear. This practice continued through the war years, but other printed fabrics were also available. Not all scrap quilts were made from feed sacks, and all poorly made yard goods were not feed sacks, either. Some poorly made fabric was sold off the bolt at dry-goods stores, and some nice fabrics were used for feed, flour, and sugar sacks.

Labels from feed sacks were sometimes printed directly on the bag and sometimes on paper labels. Occasionally, you can find a sack whose paper label has not been completely removed. Some of the printed labels would not come off. A story has been told of some fine upstanding lady with sugar or flour manufacturers' sentiments still in place on her bloomers. The 1920s and 1930s do not hold a patent on recycled sacks either. Sacking was commonly used through the 1940s and until the 1960s in rural areas. Tobacco pouches, sugar sacks, etc., have been used in many quilts since the 1800s, though not as prints. Printed sacking is still available today.

Silks became less and less common in quilts, but the use of cotton sateen for an entire quilt increased. Rayon was increasingly used in clothing, which showed up in quilts. Rayon and cotton blends, along with other man-made fibers, were developed during these years, and they slowly filtered into public use.

Occasionally, wools can be found, but mostly in tied comforters or much-prized Amish quilts. Wool quilts from this era were most often made of squares or rectangles and were sometimes made from men's suit sample books. Homespun fabrics went out of fashion and were less used, but they can be found in conjunction with wools in comforters or plain crazy quilts, "brick work," and heavy comforters with flannel backs.

Bark cloth, often used for furnishings, contained large florals and botanicals, some inspired by Hawaiian or Polynesian designs. Bark cloth was hardly useful for dresses because it would be most uncomfortable, but it appears in some utility quilts.

QUILT STYLES

Piecing patterns from the 1920s and 1930s were still available during this time, having been published and collected avidly by women all over the country during the quilt revival of the 1920s and 1930s. Pieced patterns were used to create quilts in all subsequent years. While the earlier quilts were made with clearly delineated pattern piecing, the fabrics in the quilts of the late 1940s and 1950s period often featured such busy mixtures of prints that it was difficult to tell where the block ended and the sashing components began.

Restful areas in quilt design were most often achieved by a liberal use of a white, muslin, or other solid ground. Color-coordinated pieced or appliquéd blocks of solids with a print of the same main color family became common. They were set with light grounds and used to break up the busy prints. Scrap quilts with identical pieced blocks, and with sashing cut from just one fabric, were also popular. These quilts are great examples of how the placement of light and dark fabrics can create the illusion that the blocks are all different.

Embroidery, especially French knots, buttonhole stitch, and outline stitch had a new day. Appliqué with black buttonhole stitching around each element was the most distinctive. This design feature remained until the 1950s, when it fell out of favor. It has seen a resurgence in 1990s primitive-style quilts. Much of the appliqué was stylized or simplistic. Starting in the 1920s and 1930s and continuing to the present, Sunbonnet Sue, Overall Sam, Bill, and Jim were common figures, which were appliquéd with the buttonhole stitch. Pansies and butterflies were popular in the 1950s as appliqué motifs.

Some appliquéd quilts had design elements featuring only solid fabrics with color-coordinated embroidered accents. This was particularly true of kit quilts, which often contained various solid fabrics for shading the floral designs. The kits frequently came with the quilting or appliqué outlines printed in blue, which did not wash out. Kit quilts are known for their wide-open background fields of solid white or pastel, appliquéd with floral elements. Some kits copied quilts from the 1800s. Kits and patterns were available through the mail from newspaper advertisements and catalog companies like Herrschner, Paragon, Bucilla, and Mountain Mist (Stearns & Foster).

Embroidery cross-stitch kits were available for blocks or complete quilts during the 1950s. The kits featured floral designs or sampler-style work. Crewel-work kits were also available, and some were pieced into quilts, but they were more prevalent in the 1960s.

Also popular were fund-raiser quilts with embroidered names. They were used for churches as well as ladies' groups, such as lodges. Friendship quilts, with only one or two names embroidered on each block and often containing many members of the same family, made a nice memento. They were promoted through ladies' magazines and newspapers. Lettering from this period was most often done in outline-stitch embroidery, closely followed in popularity by chain stitching.

One more thing to identify from late in this era is the painted quilt. Fabric printed with designs, much like embroidery stamping, was available for painting florals, animals, stylized colonial ladies, etc. Sometimes, the stamping would wash out and sometimes not. This fad continued into the 1960s and early 1970s and the supplies are still available today through catalog and craft stores. The stamped designs rarely have dates and are indistinguishable from the ones available in the 1960s and 1970s. In the 1940s and 1950s, a few quilts were hand painted to provide shading on solid-color fabrics. The use of tubes of paint with ballpoint tips known as liquid embroidery was popular in the late 1950s and early 1960s. Quilts that utilized crayons or wax pencils to create designs were also made. These are rare, but some do exist.

Quilts made for art's sake provided a creative outlet enjoyed by many women. Pictorial theme quilts became more common. Many unique and individual designs were inspired by the Century of Progress competition in 1933. In the early 1930s, a few women made quilts depicting the United States map.

Cotton sateens were sometimes used in appliqués, giving them an added shimmer and elegant quality because of the fabric's nap which reflects light. Sateen was also used for whole-cloth quilts or spreads that were made to match an appliqué quilt. Sateen quilts are likely to be from the 1930s or early 1940s. Many an old order Amish or Mennonite quilt was made with cotton sateen, particularly in the Midwest.

The majority of battings in this era were made of thin cotton. They were purchased from a general store or ordered from a mail-order house, such as Sears Roebuck or J.C. Penney. Battings were also made from cotton flannel sheets, woolen blankets, or older worn-out quilts. Woolen battings are rare, though they were usually associated with satin quilts.

White quilting thread was used most often, though some quilts contain thread to match the quilt's main color theme or a particular motif.

Many quilts of this period contained a moderate amount of quilting, which was a main design element. Kit quilts often featured floral motifs or feather work. Sometimes, floral motifs in the appliqué were repeated in the quilting design. Decorative quilting was used more in the 1930s than in the quilts later in this period. Fan quilting was more common in the 1940s. Many quilts, sometimes referred to as comforters, were tied with rug warping, yarn, or string.

The end of this period shows a decline in skill of the general quilt-making public. Perhaps this was caused by the increasing age of the skilled quiltmakers and subsequent failure of their eyesight and dexterity, or a decline in general interest level. In the 1960s and 1970s, a renewal of interest in hand work and in early American crafts started the quilt revival of the 1980s and 1990s.

Purples.

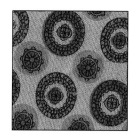

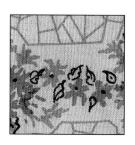

Pinks.

Rose pinks and burgundy.

Surface printed burgundy. Typical 1940s.

Reds, 1940–1950.

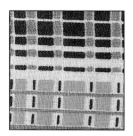

Oranges, 1930–1960.

Golden yellows and lemon yellows.

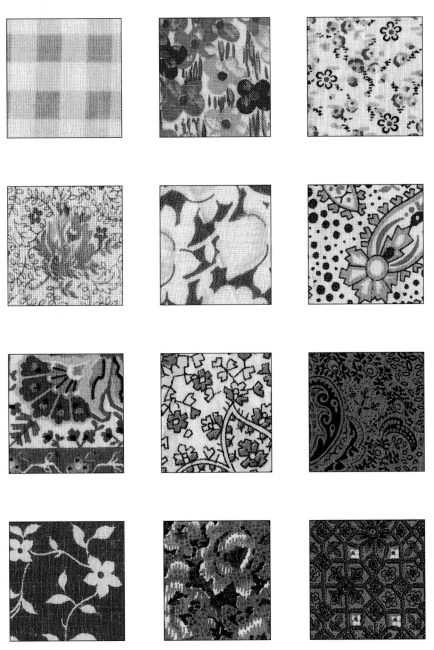

Yellows, tans, and brown-yellow combinations.

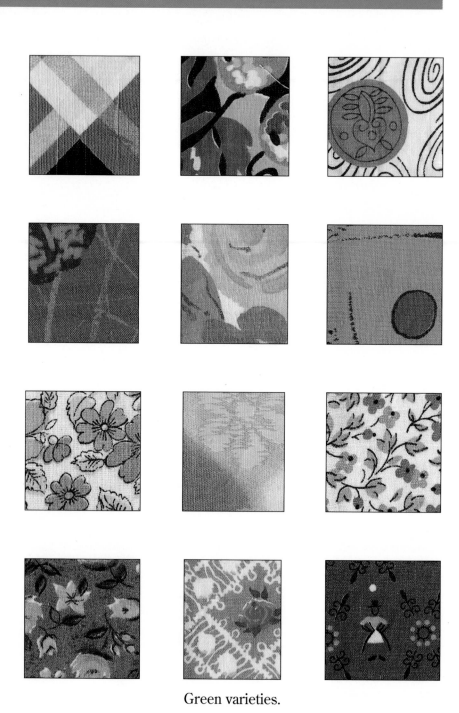

Green varieties.

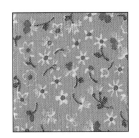

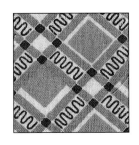

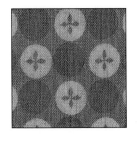

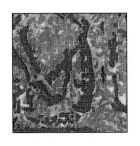

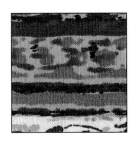

Aqua green.

Blue greens.

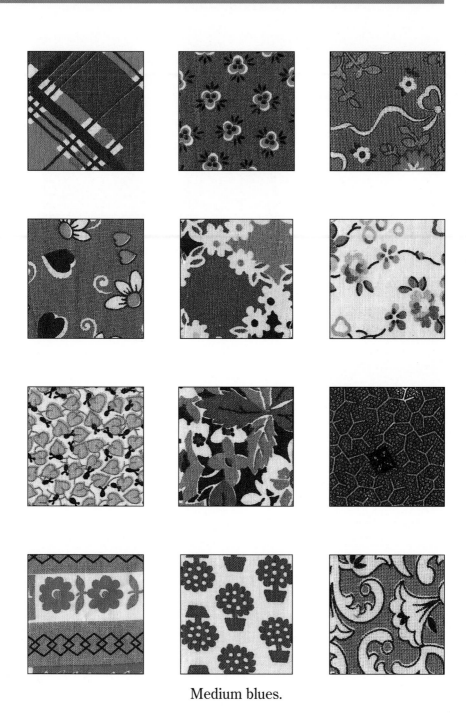

Medium blues.

Navy.

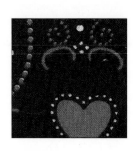

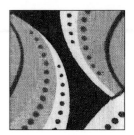

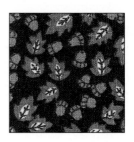

Blacks.

Grays and silver grays.

RESOURCES

DEALERS

I have found these dealers at shows and through word of mouth, and I have personally had dealings with them, particularly when they had an item I just couldn't pass by. Each business is special in its own way, and I feel confident in recommending them for their honesty and quality service.

Delectable Mountain Quilts (Marti and Bill Wivell)
6405 Biscayne Blvd.
Minneapolis, MN 55436
(612) 938-0557 (leave message)
E-mail: mwivell@classic.msn.com
Lots of goodies! Beautiful quilts, sewing implements, other interesting whimsies. Not many small pieces.

Diane Reese
PO Box 598
Townsend, ME 01469
(978) 433-9174
Early pieces of chintz and other great scraps. Yardage of some very early 1800 pieces. Sometimes, some late 1700 things, too.

Jean Lyle
PO Box 289
Quincy, IL 62306
(217) 222-8910
E-mail: JSlyle@BCL.net
Carries some interesting pre-1940 tops and quilts. Scrap bags of pre-1940 fabrics, especially the 1860–1890 period. Also sells crepeline, Orvus, and new sewing implements.

Joe and Mary Koval Antiques
Box 550, Lutz School Rd.
Indiana, PA 15701
(724) 465-7370
E-mail: mkfabrics@microserve.net
Possibly the greatest collection of pre-1900 fabrics for sale by the foot
or the fat quarter. Great scrap bags of fabric, blocks, linens, and relat-
ed textiles. Beautiful quilts and tops, too, but the unadulterated fabrics are what draw me back time and time again.

John Sauls' Antiques
Box 448, 310 W. Rusk
Tyler, TX 75710
(903) 593-4668
E-mail: johnsauls@Tyler.net
Blocks, tops, and quilts of all varieties, from orphans to grand beauties. The rare and lovely are likely to be found. Laces, rag rugs, coverlets and other whimsies. "By chance or appointment," but usually
quick to return messages.

Kirk Collection (Bill and Nancy Kirk)
1513 Military Ave.
Omaha, NE 68111
(402) 551-0386 or (800) 398-2542
E-mail: kirkcoll@aol.com
www.kirkcollection.com
1820–1960 fabrics by the yard and scrap bags. Exceptional collection
of fabrics from early 1900–1960. Prompt mail-order service will try to
match your requirements. Quilting notions, books, and high quality
reproductions.

Labors of Love
PO Box 352
Hillsdale, NY 12520
(518) 325-6468
Beautiful early 1800 quilts. They usually have a large selection of
them on hand.

Legacy Quilts (Xenia Cord)
2217 Avalon Ct.
Kokomo, IN 46902
(765) 453-2547
E-mail: xecord@netusa1.net
Quilts, tops, vintage fabrics. By appointment only and at shows.

Log Cabin Quilts (Mary Ann Walters)
4200 Peggy Ln.
Plano, TX 75074
(972) 881-2818
E-mail: logcabin@flashnet
www.flash.net/~logcabin
Good assorted collection of nice quilts, often very graphic. Usually has blocks and tops as well. By appointment only and at shows.

Cindy's Quilts (Cindy Rennels)
Box 1212
Clinton, OK 73601
(580) 323-1174
A large collection of quilts and blocks to choose from. Usually late 1800 through 1900. Lots of midwest 1900.

ORGANIZATIONS

These organizations offer quilt shows in varied venues, provide classes in quilt history, or provide information that you may be seeking. Most have memberships that you can join to learn more about quilts and quilt history.

American Quilt Study Group
660 Mission St.
San Francisco, CA 94105-4007
(415) 495-0163
E-mail: AQSG@aol.com

American Quilter's Society
PO Box 3290
Paducah, KY 42002-3290
(502) 898-7903
http://www.AQSquilt.com

Crazy Quilt Society
PO Box 19452
Omaha, NE 68119
(402) 551-0368 or (800) 599-0094
www.crazyquilt.com

International Quilt Association
7660 Woodway, Suite 550
Houston, TX 77063
(713) 781-6864
www.quilts.com

National Quilt Association
PO Box 393
Ellicott City, MD 21041-0393
(410) 461-5733
http://www.his.com.queenb/nqa

Professional Association of Appraisers–Quilted Textiles
c/o AQS
PO Box 3290
Paducah, KY 42002-3290

Quilt Heritage Foundation
PO Box 19452
Omaha, NE 68119
(402) 551-0386 or (800) 599-0094
E-mail: Quilthf@aol.com
www.quiltheritage.com

Quilt Restoration Society
PO Box 19452
Omaha, NE 68119
www.quiltrestoration.com

Vintage Quilt & Textile Society
2401 Blue Cypress
Richardson, TX 75082
(972) 783-4149
E-mail: VQTS1@airmail.net

Feed Sack Club
25 S. Starr Ave. #16
Pittsburgh, PA 15202
(412) 766-3996

MUSEUMS

This is a short list of some of the museums across the United States
which have textile collections. Seeing the quilts and other textiles in
their collections is very helpful in learning about older quilts. Most
museums have a textile curator or other staff member who may be
able to refer you to some assistance in your own area.

American Craft Museum
40 W. 53rd St.
New York, NY 10019-6136
(212) 956-3535

Charleston Museum
360 Meeting St.
Charleston, SC 29403
(803) 733-2996

Daughters of the American Revolution
1776 D St. NW

Washington, DC 20006
(202) 879-3208

Decatur House Museum
748 Jackson Pl. NW
Washington, DC 20006
(202) 842-0920

New England Quilt Museum
18 Shattuck St.
Lowell, MA 01952
(978) 452-4207

San Jose Amercian Museum of Quilts and Textiles
60 S. Market St.
San Jose, CA
(408) 971-0323

Shelburne Museum
PO Box 10
Shelburne, VT 05482
(802) 985-3346

St. Louis Art Museum
#1 Fine Arts Dr.
St. Louis, MO 63110

Rocky Mountain Quilt Museum
1111 Washington
Golden, CO 80401
(303) 277-0377

Museum of the American Quilter's Society
PO Box 1540
Paducah, KY 42002-1540
(502) 442-8856

Peoples' Place Museum
Rte. 340
Intercourse, PA 17534
(800) 828-8218

Old Sturbridge Village
1 Old Sturbridge Village Rd.
Sturbridge, MA 01566
(508) 347-3362

GLOSSARY

Alternate block – A large, unpieced square of fabric set between appliquéd or pieced blocks in a quilt. In 1850-era quilts, alternate blocks were often heavily quilted with a variety of decorative patterns and sometimes contained stuffed work to create a relief design.

Aniline dyes – Chemical dyes (as opposed to vegetable dyes) derived from coal tar. These were developed beginning in the late 1850s and included mauvine purple and alizarin crimson.

Apprentice – Usually male, an apprentice was contracted by his parents to work for and serve a skilled craftsman or tradesman. In exchange for the years of service, the young man was expected to learn the trade of the master. Apprenticeship usually terminated at the young man's 21st birthday. Twenty-one was the age at which a boy was considered a man, and freedom quilts were sometimes made to celebrate this birthday.

Broderie perse – (Loosely translated: Persian embroidery.) A type of quilt or quilt block featuring decorative motifs cut from chintz or other large-scale print and appliquéd in a decorative pattern. These quilts frequently feature buttonhole embroidery around the edges.

Butterscotch – A golden yellow print consisting of an overall printing of small chrome yellow paste prints. The pattern looks solid yellow at a distance. (See Double Pinks.)

By the piece – Quilting lines follow the seam lines of pieced patches at a certain distance from the seams.

Chambray – Woven fabric made from a white warp and a colored weft, familiar currently in light or medium blue. It was popular in a variety of colors at the turn of the twentieth century.

Cheddar orange – Chrome orange of a distinctive cheddar cheese color, popular in the last quarter of the 1800s. (See Chrome Yellow.)

Chinoserie – Fabric print styles produced in Europe or for the European market, based on print motifs or themes from China and the Far East.

Chrome yellow – A bright yellow dye created from chromate of lead (lead sugar). This dyestuff was also used to create chrome orange. Chromate of lead is hazardous and no longer used in textile production. Chrome yellow or orange was used as a dye or a paste for printing, which created a raised surface print, most common on dark indigo blue or Turkey red fabrics. Chrome yellow may become fugitive suddenly and bleed onto other fabrics, so items dyed with it should be stored separately. Chrome orange and chrome yellow may corrode to greenish shades. These can often be washed to remove the green.

Chrome orange – (See Chrome yellow or Cheddar.)

Conversation prints – Designs that were usually printed on a white or solid-colored ground and featured a recognizable object as the motif. Some examples would be horseshoes and whips, foxes in hats, bumblebees, or bugs that are anatomically correct. These are frequently referred to as object prints. Produced from mid-1800s onward and possibly much sooner, they are most well known in the 1880–1910 period.

Double print – A print made by printing several layers of pink, rose, or red over one another to create the appearance at a distance of a solid color, but on close examination a textured pink can be seen. The same technique was used to create Lancaster blues, butterscotch (with chrome yellow), purples, and browns. Some double purples change to brown. Double pinks and purples often have a regular pattern of unprinted areas creating a white space. Double pinks are sometimes referred to as cinnamon pinks, though some believe there is a difference. These were printed from the 1850s through the early 1900s and were being made as reproduction prints in the 1980s and 1990s.

Double-rodded – (Also Triple-rodded.) A standard quilt appraiser's and quilt dealer's term for two parallel lines of quilting stitches separated by a space then repeated across the surface of the quilt, usually at a diagonal. Double-rodded quilting lines are usually straight, but they may also be wavy. Used as a fill pattern for quilting.

Fondue prints – (See Ombré.)

Friendship quilt – A quilt that features signatures of a variety of people, either in ink, stamping, or embroidery. These quilts were most popular during the 1840–1850 period and again in the mid to late 1930s. Quilts prior to 1850 were likely to have cross-stitch signatures similar to other household linens. Often these signatures were stitched with the makers own hair. The 1840–1860 quilts were more likely to have inked signatures and dates. Quilts from the 1850s are also known as album quilts. Quilts from the 1930s usually have signatures worked in outline stitch or chain stitch embroidery. Blocks may have identical patterns or a variety of piecing. Appliqué patterns sometimes appear in these quilts.

Fugitive – An unstable dye that tends to run, fade, or change colors. Sometimes a fugitive dye will bleed onto nearby fabrics.

Fustic – A tree of the mulberry family.

Ghost fabric – A fabric in which the dye was fugitive, leaving no color or only a little color in a seam. This condition is most often seen in some red and green appliqué quilts from the late 1800s and some pinks and blues from the 1910–1920 era.

Indiennes – Fabric print styles loosely based on print motifs reminiscent of India and copied in Europe or India for the European market.

Indigo – A plant grown for its dyeing properties and used to produce a multitude of blues. Indigo was also used with other dyes to create greens and purples and give depth of color to some black shades. Indigo is the oldest known dependable dye colorant. It was used to dye some fabrics found in Egyptian tombs. Every continent has a plant that will produce the same chemical compound as indigo. An artificial indigo was developed in the late 1800s, though some countries still use the original plant. Indigo prints are being made in Africa, Japan, Eastern Europe, and the United States. Indigo-dyed fabrics have a distinctive scent before being washed, a smell rumored to be repulsive to snakes. Artificial indigo is now used to dye fibers for denim blue jeans.

In the ditch – Quilting lines as close to the seams as possible.

Lancaster blue – A small print consisting of one or more layers of blue to create the appearance of an overall bright clear blue, which on close examination reveals a fine print. It is sometimes referred to as Pennsylvania blue or double blue and was especially prevalent in Pennsylvania quilts from the last half of the 1800s. When wet, this blue usually turns a soft blue-gray, which never returns to the original bright blue.

Madder – A shrubby herb grown for the dyeing properties of its root. Madder is the basic colorant for Turkey red and the coppery browns of the 1860s and 1870s. With different mordants, the plant produces purple, pink, red, orange, and several browns.

Madras cloth – Patterns used by expert weavers and dyers in Madras, India. These designs have remained the same for centuries. Derived from natural vegetable dyes, the colors are sometimes fugitive, but they are soft pastel to clear and bright, without being garish. Madras is a soft, yarn-dyed woven cotton cloth that breathes. The fabrics made in India today are indistinguishable from cloth made 200 years ago.

Medallion – A quilt style with a prominent central motif, usually surrounded by several pieced borders, additional appliqué elements, or elaborate quilting designs. Broderie perse quilts from the late 1700s and early 1800s featuring a large central tree are good examples of this style of quilt, as are 1920–1950 quilts made from kits featuring stylized floral elements in the center.

Mordant – A mineral salt which aids in setting dye colors to make them colorfast on fabrics and which alters the shades of dyes by chemical reaction. Different mordants will create different colors with the same dyestuff.

Mosaic – Quilt piecing containing hexagons or 60-degree diamonds, reminiscent of mosaic tile floors and walls of the Middle East. These designs usually feature stars, boxes, or concentric-circle patterns. Earlier versions (pre-1850) often feature wide chintz borders. The 1860–1890 versions may be made entirely of silk and brocades or ribbons with much black for contrast with the brilliant colors. After 1900, these were commonly made with pastel or bright cottons with white, or sometimes with the addition of green triangles. They were usually pieced in rosettes after 1900 and are known to us as Grandmother's Flower Garden quilts.

Object Prints – (See Conversation prints.)

Ombré – A technique for printing gradations of the same color from pastel to dark and back again. It often includes more than one color on the same fabric in varied shades, along either the width, the length, or both. Vivid blues, reds, purples, or greens were used in the 1820–1850 period, with wide stripes (four–six inches). The 1860–1890 ombré prints usually have a narrow stripe (one inch), and tend to have more subdued colors, such as rose, browns, dusky green, or old-gold. Also known as rainbow or fondue prints, these have been reproduced in the late 1980s and early 1990s as fabric lines representing 1850s fabrics.

On Point – A pieced or appliquéd square set into a quilt with a point at the top, creating a diamond shape. Quilts set on point usually require triangles at the sides and corners to make a square or rectangular quilt.

Overdyed – A piece of yard goods that was vat dyed in two different baths to create a third color, e.g., indigo blue and quercitron yellow to make an overdyed green. Often, one or the other color will be fugitive and leave streaks. These colors may have appeared the same at one time, but if they have faded unevenly, the greens may no longer match. Surface printing and resist techniques were sometimes used with overdyeing to create secondary patterns.

Penciling – The practice of hand painting portions of yard goods with colors or details that were not achieved in the dyeing or printing processes. Women and children were hired at low wages to perform this tedious task.

Picotage – Tiny, closely spaced dots in a fabric print, creating background texture or shading in a pattern. These dots were created with small nails or pins pounded into wooden blocks or by fine raised points on copper plates or copper rollers.

Quercitron – Inner part of bark of North American black oak, containing tannin.

Resist – A protective coating, stitching or tying of fabric, or applying a starchy paste or wax with the intention of preventing a piece of fabric from absorbing dye in a certain area when immersed in a dye bath.

Rainbow prints – (See Ombré.)

Sash and post – Strips of fabrics that separate pieced or appliquéd blocks and which have a small square in the corners where the blocks join. The square may or may not be a different color, or it may feature a pieced square or an individual quilt design to enhance the main blocks.

Sashing – Strips of fabric sewn between blocks to join them, giving a lattice effect.

Shirting prints – Woven fabrics with a white or off-white ground and small motifs, either geometrics, stripes, or object prints in regular patterns across the surface. Very popular from 1880 to 1920, these fabrics were also produced much earlier in the 1800s, but they seem to have been overlooked by many fabric historians.

Strippie – A quilt piecing style featuring pieced blocks set together, often on point with triangle fills, to create strips. The strips are then sewn together alternating with strips of fabric to create a quilt top which often has no additional border. These quilts were common along the eastern seaboard and in Pennsylvania from 1800 through 1830 and in the 1860s and 1870s.

Surface print – A color or motif that appears only on one side of a finished piece of yard goods. Some bleed-through may occur, but the fabric has an obvious right and wrong side. A surface print may be vat dyed as well as surface-printed, leaving the motif clear only on the right side of the fabric. Surface-printed background colors are often a good identifying factor for distinguishing some reproduction prints from vintage fabrics.

Tendering – To weaken fabric through chemical action. Many dyes in the brown and black color ranges were made from such caustic substances that the fabrics are extremely fragile. Many weaves have lost their black or brown stripes. Printed dots or other figures have fallen away, leaving holes like Swiss cheese. Entire lengths of fabric will crumble in your hands. Some of these corrosive substances are lye, iron rust, and gall.

Trapunto – A term commonly used in the 1980s and 1990s to describe the use of stuffed quilting motifs that create relief patterns on a quilt surface. Stuffed work may be created in a number of ways. Stuffed work was very popular for fine quilts of the 1850 era, as part of white-work whole-cloth quilts, or for the alternate blocks of red and green quilts or blue and white quilts.

Triple-rodded – (See Double-rodded.)

Turkey red – A specific shade of red produced from the madder plant. The technique involved placing fabric in an oil bath (rumored to have been boiled for nine days). A colorfast dye, it was used in the Ottomon Empire extensively, hence the name. Pre-1812, it might have been printed with black or yellow. In 1812 through the 1850s, it was often printed with blue, green, black, and yellow. After the 1850s it was more commonly a plain solid red. Turkey red fades to pink after use as the outer layers become worn, and it shreds after much use.

Vegetable dyes – Dyes that use plant matter in combination with various mordants to create many colors.

Vermiculate patterns – Small squiggly lines created by wood print blocks with metal strips or by copper plates or copper rollers. Very popular in late 1700 and early 1800 prints, this type of pattern is similar to quilting designs in early English quilts (backstitched) and in 1990s machine-quilted quilts as a fill pattern.

Weld – A European mignonette plant that yields a yellow dye.

Whole cloth – A style of quilt made from lengths or sections of cloth of the same type and color, and quilted. Most notable are the indigo blue wool calimanco quilts of the late 1700s and early 1800s, the whitework of the 1850s, and the satin whole-cloths of the 1930s. Whole-cloth whitework quilts are likely to have had white tied-fringe edges.

Woad – Plants of the crucifer family used to produce dyes.

BIBLIOGRAPHY

Adrosko, Rita J., *Natural Dyes and Home Dying*, Dover Publications, New York, NY, 1971.

Allen and Tuckhorn, *A Maryland Album*, Rutledge Hill Press, Nashville, TN, 1995.

Barber, Rita, *Somewhere In Between – Quilts and Quilters of Illinois*, American Quilter's Society, Paducah, KY, 1986.

Bemiss, Elijah, *A Dyer's Companion*, reprinted by General Publishing for Dover Publishing, Toronto, Canada, 1973.

Boscene, Susan, *Hand Block Printing and Resist Dying*, David and Charles Publisher, Brunel House, Newton Abbot, Devon, England, 1991.

Bosker, Mancini, and Gramstad, *Fabulous Fabrics of the Fifties (and Other Terrific Textiles of the 20's, 30's, and 40's)*, Chronicle Books, San Francisco, CA, 1992.

Brackman, Barbara, *Clues in the Calico – A Guide to Identifying and Dating Antique Quilts*, EPM Publications, McLean, VA, 1989.

Brackman and Waldvogel, *A Century of Progress – Patchwork Souvenirs of the 1933 World's Fair*, Rutledge Hill Press, Nashville, TN, 1993.

Bredif, Josette, *Printed French Fabrics – Toiles De Jouy*, Rizzoli

(American Publisher), New York, NY, Thames and Hudson, (English Translation), Editions Adam Biro (French Editions), 1989.

Bullard and Shiell, *Chintz Quilts: Unfading Glory*, Serendipity Publishers, Tallahassee, FL, 1983.

Oklahoma Quilt Heritage Project, *Oklahoma Heritage Quilts*, American Quilter's Society, Paducah, KY, 1990.

Christensen, Erwin O., *Index of American Design*, 3rd edition, Macmillan, Toronto, Canada, 1967.

Clark, Knepper and Ronsheim, *Quilts in Community – Ohio's Traditions*, Rutledge Hill Press, Nashville, TN, 1991.

Colby, Averil, *Patchwork*, Charles Scribner and Sons, New York, NY, 1971.

Colby, Averil, *Quilting*, Charles Scribner and Sons, New York, NY, 1971.

Delineator Magazine, Philadelphia, PA, July, 1865.

Handwoven Textiles of India, Mapin Publishing for Grantha Corporation, Middletown, NJ, 1989.

The Heritage Quilt Project of New Jersey, *New Jersey Quilts 1777–1950 – Contributions To An American Tradition*, American Quilter's Society, Paducah, KY, 1992.

Indiana Quilt Registry Project, *Quilts of Indiana – Crossroads of Memories*, Indiana University Press, Bloomington and Indianapolis, IN, 1991.

Kiracofe, Roderick, *The American Quilt*, Clarkson Potter Publishers, New York, NY, 1993.

Kolter, Jane Bentley, *Forget Me Not – A Gallery of Friendship and Album Quilts*, The Main Street Press, Pittstown, NJ, 1985.

Ladies Friend Magazine, April 1870, Vol. XII, Issue 4-17, Deacon and Peterson Publishing, Philadelphia, PA.

Ladies Gallery Magazine, Vol. 2, Issue 6, Boghouse Publishing, Independence, MO.

Lasansky, Jeannette, *In the Heart Of Pennsylvania – 19th and 20th Century Quiltmaking Traditions*, Oral Traditions Project, Lewisburg, PA, 1985.

Lavitt and Weissman, *Labors of Love – America's Textile and Needlework 1650–1930*, Wings Books, Avenel, NJ.

Martin, Nancy J., *Pieces of the Past*, That Patchwork Place, Bothell, WA, 1986.

Martin, Nancy J., *Threads of Time*, That Patchwork Place, Bothell, WA, 1990.

McMorris, Penny, *Crazy Quilts*, E.P. Dutton, New York, NY, 1984.

Mellers and Elffers, *Textile Designs*, Harry N. Abrams, Inc., New York, NY, 1991.

Montgomery, Florence, *Textiles in America*, 1650–1870, 1974.

Nephew, Sara, *My Mother's Quilts – Designs from the Thirties*, That Patchwork Place, Bothell, WA, 1988.

Newman, Joyce Jaines, *North Carolina Quilts*, The University of North Carolina Press, Chapel Hill, NC, 1988.

Parry, Linda, *William Morris Textiles*, Viking Press, New York, NY, 1983.

Pellman and Pellman, *A Treasury of Mennonite Quilts*, Good Books, Intercourse, PA, 1992.

Pellman and Pellman, *The World of Amish Quilts*, Good Books, Intercourse, PA, 1984.

Perry and Frolli, *A Joy Forever – Marie Webster's Quilt Patterns*, Practical Patchwork, Santa Barbara, CA, 1992.

Pettit, Florence, *America's Printed and Painted Textiles 1600–1900*, Hastings House, New York, NY, 1970.

Rae, Janet, *The Quilts Of the British Isles*, Bellew Publishing Co. Ltd., London, England, 1987.

Ramsey and Waldvogel, *The Quilts of Tennessee – Images of Domestic Life Prior to 1930*, Rutledge Hill Press, Nashville, TN, 1986.

Safford and Bishop, *America's Quilts and Coverlets*, Bonanza Books, New York, NY, 1980.

Sandberg, Gosta, *Indigo Textiles – Technique and History*, Norstedts Forlag, Stockholm, Sweden, 1986, A and C Black Ltd., Publishers, London, England, and Lark Books, Asheville, NC, 1989.

———. *The Red Dyes – Cochineal, Madder, and Murex Purple*, Norstedts Forlag, Stockholm, Sweden, 1994, A and C Black Ltd., Publishers, London, England, and Lark Books, Asheville, NC, 1997.

Schoeser, Mary, *Fabrics and Wallpapers – Twentieth Century Design*, Bell and Hyman, London, England, 1986.

Schoeser and Rufey, *English and American Textiles from 1790 to the Present*, Thames and Hudson, New York, NY, 1989.

Sears Catalog of 1897, edited by Fred L. Isreal, Chelsea House Publishing, New York, NY and Philadelphia, PA, excerpt reprinted in 1993.

Sears Catalog of 1902, Gramercy Books, Avenel, NJ, excerpt reprinted in 1993.

Sears Catalog of 1908, edited by Joseph Schroeder, Jr., DBI Books, Northbrook, IL, 1969.

Storey, Joyce, *The Thames and Hudson Manual of Dyes and Fabrics*, Thames and Hudson, London, England, 1978, 1985, 1992.

Strachey, Lytton, *Queen Victoria*, Chatto and Windus Publisher, London, England, reprinted 1993.

Tomlonson, Judy Schroeder, *Mennonite Quilts and Pieces*, Good Books, Intercourse, PA, 1985.

Victoria And Albert Museum Textile Collection, *Designs for Printed Textiles in England 1750–1850*, Abbeyville Press, New York, NY, 1992.

Von Gwinner, Schnuppe, *The History of the Patchwork Quilt*, (Translated from German by Dr. Edward Force), Schiffer Publishing, West Chester, PA, 1988.

Waldvogel, Merikay, S*oft Covers For Hard Times – Quiltmaking & The Great Depression*, Rutledge Hill Press, Nashville, TN, 1990.

Williams, Charlotte Allen, *Florida Quilts*, University Press of Florida, Gainesville, FL, 1992.

Wingate, Isabel, *Textile Fabrics and Their Selection*, 7th Edition, Prentiss-Hall, Inc., Englewood Cliffs, NJ, 1976.

Woodward and Greenstein, *Twentieth Century Quilts 1900–1950*, E.P. Dutton, New York, NY, 1989.

About the Author

Eileen Jahnke Trestain was raised in a small town outside Grand Rapids, Michigan. She has always spent much of her time in art and craft pursuits. At the age of 10, her grandmother introduced her to quilting, which began a lifelong interest.

In 1984, Eileen married, and she and her husband, David, moved to Dallas, Texas. There, she worked as a floral designer, specializing in silk and dried floral arrangements. She continued her interest in quilting and began to collect and study quilting patterns.

After moving to Plano, Texas, in 1988, she joined the Quilter's Guild of Plano. Shortly thereafter, she was invited to assist the Heritage Farmstead in cataloging quilts in the county. Eileen coordinated the recording and photographing of more than 450 quilts in the Collin County, Texas, area over the next two years. The project, with the assistance of guild members, culminated in an exhibit at the Heritage Farmstead Museum.

With the encouragement of friends, Eileen began producing her own line of patterns under the business name of Peonies Needlework Crafts. Her patterns feature three-dimensional appliqué, traditional appliqué, and piecing elements. She began to teach in local shops, and soon, she was teaching nationally. In 1993, she was awarded the First Prize in the Master/Professional Quilter category, at the Dallas Quilt Celebration, for her "Rosie O'Grady" jacket. It featured her technique for dimensional appliqué and Celtic interlace.

Eileen took the course in appraising quilts offered by the American Quilter's Society in 1991. In 1992, she passed the certification exams to become a Certified Appraiser of Quilted Textiles. After moving to Arizona in 1994, Eileen served as the coordinator for the Q.U.I.L.T. Education program for the Arizona Quilter's Guild, and she was founding president for the Phoenix Area Quilters Association.

Special Books by AQS

Keep the history of your quilts alive with these organizers offered by AQS. These memory-keepers allow you to preserve not only the financial value of your quilt, but also the emotional value.

◀ PROTECTING YOUR QUILTS

Perfect for protecting your investment in old and new quilts and qulit-related textiles. Information on protecting and caring for quilts, types of insurance needed, list of conservation supplies, and a glossary are provided. Revised edition. 5½" x 8½".

32 pages, **#4779** **$6.95**

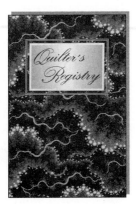

QUILTER'S REGISTRY ▶

by Lynne Fritz

An attractive, padded hardbound cover provides extra protection for your records and photographs of all your quilts. Includes space for photos, dimensions, technical information, and details for each item. 5½" x 8½".

80 pages, **#2380** **$9.95**

◀ MY QUILT JOURNAL

A diary to write your personal thoughts about your creations, so your love for quilting can be enjoyed by many generations to come. 5" x 7".

80 pages, **#5205** **$2.95**

PERSONAL QUILT REGISTRY ▶

Filling this registry out provides satisfaction for a finished project, as well as keeping efficient records for insurance purposes and tax records. 5½" x 8½".

64 pages, **#5203** **$3.95**

For a complete listing of AQS titles, write or call: Amercian Quilter's Society, PO Box 3290, Paducah, KY 42002-3290, 800-626-5420.